The English Poor

Thomas Mackay

Cambridge
University Press

CAMBRIDGE UNIVERSITY PRESS

Cambridge, New York, Melbourne, Madrid, Cape Town, Singapore,
São Paolo, Delhi, Dubai, Tokyo

Published in the United States of America by Cambridge University Press, New York

www.cambridge.org
Information on this title: www.cambridge.org/9781108003704

This edition first published 1889
This digitally printed version 2009

ISBN 978-1-108-00370-4 Paperback

CAMBRIDGE LIBRARY COLLECTION

Books of enduring scholarly value

History

The books reissued in this series include accounts of historical events and movements by eye-witnesses and contemporaries, as well as landmark studies that assembled significant source materials or developed new historiographical methods. The series includes work in social, political and military history on a wide range of periods and regions, giving modern scholars ready access to influential publications of the past.

The English Poor

In 1889, British wine merchant Thomas Mackay published The English Poor, which espoused the ideas of Darwin and applied them to British social and economic history. An acolyte of social Darwinist Herbert Spencer, Mackay writes that human history has been a struggle between individualism and socialism, and argues that only through individual competition (not state social support) will poverty be eradicated. The opening chapters discuss the human instinct for property accumulation, primitive forms of society, elite control of workers during the plague years, and the growth of the proletariat. Later chapters discuss social legislation, the evolution of England's poor laws, and the Industrial Revolution. Finally, Mackay debates the scholarship of socialist Ernest Belfort Bax, bemoans the misguided ideas of Christian charity, and argues that the lives of 'lower types' of people have been prolonged by the poor laws. This is a fascinating document of late Victorian economic thought.

THE

ENGLISH POOR

THE ENGLISH POOR

A SKETCH OF THEIR SOCIAL AND ECONOMIC HISTORY

BY T. MACKAY

'The rich man's wealth is his strong city; the destruction of the poor is their poverty'—*The Proverbs of Solomon* x. 15

LONDON
JOHN MURRAY, ALBEMARLE STREET
1889

PREFACE

THE purpose of this work is to direct attention to the influences which have dominated the history of the poor in this country. It will be found that the view presented differs from the popularly conceived opinion as to the causes which have produced the inequalities of modern life.

Assumptions have been made without sufficient inquiry, yet of such importance that they control with disastrous effect the whole course of modern speculation, and, consequently, of modern practice. It has been assumed that Socialism is something new, and that in the past, human destiny has been entrusted to the care of the individualistic principle. The main object of the present volume is to show that this is the very contrary of the truth. The dominant principle in human affairs has been Socialism. History is the record of the gradual and painful emancipation of the individual from the socialistic tyranny of slavery, feudalism, and centralised authority.

The salient distinction between the Socialist and the Individualist theory of life, as it is understood in these pages, may here be stated. By Individualism is meant the rule of conduct which obliges each individual man to adapt his instincts, habits, and character to his surroundings. These surroundings in civilised and associated life are governed by economic laws, which though not of inflexible rigidity are yet more permanent in their nature than human character. They are indeed the environment in reference to which human character must be formed. The definition assumes that man has inherited a capacity for this course of action, a capacity which can be developed by use and transmitted with ever-growing intensity to successive generations. This to the Individualist is Nature's Covenant of Progress.

By Socialism is meant the instinct which induces men to reject, unconsciously for the most part, Nature's offer of safe conduct, and to submit themselves, in their search for happiness, to the guidance of groups and associations of men. A study of primitive ideas will show that such associations owed their first origin to the desire for giving effect to some universal superstition or wish; that by a natural process of deterioration (for the individualistic instincts of self-preservation and acquisition are ineradicable and in the long run more potent than the combining motive of association) they soon fall away from their ideal purpose and become mere close corporations working only for the benefit of those who from time to time can control the authority of the State. Such is the origin of all government that is not based on the mere right of conquest. The Socialist points to the chaos and oppression which has arisen in this conflict of opposing principles, and attributes the disorder to 'Individualism run wild.' But in his analysis of cause and effect he forgets mankind's primitive surrender to socialistic control.

These definitions disclose the line of argument which is to be followed. In the introductory chapter, with a view of obtaining a master-key to the situation, appeal is made to the modern doctrine of Evolution. The preference given to an individualistic basis of society is supported by this, the greatest scientific discovery of the century. For, beyond all dispute, in the world of creation it is to individual organisms and not to groups and associations of these that Nature has confided the secret of progress, the power of self-adjustment to environment. The argument goes on to show that property, wealth, or the surplus of maintenance over and above what is necessary for the hand-to-mouth life of a savage, is a main part of the environment of civilisation. To this mankind has to adjust itself.

It becomes, then, a pertinent question to ask—To which of the rival motives of action has man yielded in his dealing with the tenure and distribution of property? An answer is given in the text, and it will appear that in some of the most important crises of the history of property man has surrendered to his socialistic impulses. Notably this has been the case with regard to land, for long the most important item in the country's wealth; indeed, while the laws against usury continued to restrict the larger operations of trade, it would hardly be an exaggeration to call land the sole form of national capital. As far, therefore, as English history is concerned, the feudal tenure of land is described as the most noteworthy instance of socialistic usurpation.

The attempt to establish these propositions will bring the reader to a brief consideration of the Village Community, the Villenage of the feudal manor, and of the somewhat analogous institutions of the town—the Merchant and Craft Gilds of mediæval life. Some description will be given of the struggle of the labourer to free himself from the serfdom which resulted from this dedication of property, his means of progress and survival, to the maintenance of a stereotyped form of Socialism. It will be seen how he emerged from the struggle, with his character warped and with his acquisitive instincts atrophied by disuse; how he was then delivered, unarmed, so to speak, to the mighty forces of modern Industrialism.

At length the inquiry brings us to the problem of to-day. The difficulty of the situation is enormous, and Society stands halting between two opinions.

The larger proposals of the thorough-going Socialist seem condemned by the experience of the past. His demand is for the endowment of democratic Socialism and the permanent maintenance of a state of society in which all gain their living by labour. To the present governing class, the workmen of England, such an ideal, impracticable though it may be, has its attraction; but in a world of evolution and progress all human ideals are of necessity evanescent. Already there are signs of a writing on the wall. The every-day-increasing substitution of machinery for manual labour, and the straits to which unskilled labour is put to compete with it, might suggest to one who wished to play the prophet, a new ideal.

But it is more difficult to find an answer to those less logical but more plausible advocates who recommend an extension of the duties and responsibilities of the State. With them the matter must be argued out in detail. State socialistic action seems to promise so much. The order to stand aside and let Nature assert herself seems so cynical and cruel. Even if the correctness of the diagnosis here presented is admitted, it may still be argued that the disease is to be cured by further application of socialistic remedies.

With a view of throwing light on this remaining doubt, it has seemed necessary to make a brief examination of some of the more prominent enterprises of the limited State Socialism under which we live.

Practical politicians may differ as to the temporary necessity of such measures, and no sane man will urge indiscriminate or wholesale changes in existing legislation; but in the long run it should be borne in mind that every attempt on the part of the State to distribute economical advantages or property by any means other than by the free play of the individual instincts of self-preservation and acquisition, is unsatisfactory and incomplete. It is *unsatisfactory* in that, excuse it as we may, it is essentially an endowment of incompetence. Nature's plan is the endowment of caution, self-control, and capacity; and if men contract themselves out of this law they will lose in the end more than they gain. It is *incomplete*, for no power of man can provide adequate guarantees of happiness for those who have never learnt in Nature's school the rudimentary arts of competition and self-protection.

Such is the argument of the following pages. Of the facts it is only to be said that no claim of new discovery is put forward. The main purpose is to supply a true interpretation of facts which are for the most part notorious and beyond dispute.

Those who accept this diagnosis of disease are little tempted to produce a numbered schedule of panaceas, but something is gained if the disease is understood and the errors of past physicians exposed. 'Natura non nisi parendo vincitur.' Nature is the true physician; if we can but return to the guidance of her hand the future is secure.

It only remains for the author to avow his obligation to the teaching of Mr. Herbert Spencer.

As a rule, where such corroboration appears necessary, the source of information as to facts is stated in the text. Acknowledgment of indebtedness is due to Mr. Thorold Rogers' 'Six Centuries of Work and Wages' and to his 'History of Agricultural Prices.' These works are a mine of information as to the rural economy of mediæval England. For the ancient history of the Poor Law the author has relied mainly on the work of the late Sir George Nicholls, and for the modern aspect of the question the evidence of Sir H. Owen before the Select Committee of the House of Lords has been used.

CONTENTS

THE ENGLISH POOR

CHAPTER I

PROPERTY THE MAIN CONDITION OF SURVIVAL. THE GENERAL PROPOSITION STATED

THE INSTITUTION OF PROPERTY has been a principal condition of man's survival in the struggle for existence.

He has been able to produce more wealth than was needed to satisfy the wants of the passing hour. Relative to the surplus wealth so created, there has grown up in man's mind the instinct of appropriation, in its fuller development, the legalised principle of property. This has been man's most potent weapon of self-preservation. Ethnologists and jurists can supply us with some of the details of the process, for the instinct which has made property a necessity in all civilised society has been curiously interwoven with fictions of custom, religion, and law. Still out of the obscurity which surrounds the history of primitive ideas one fact stands clearly forth, namely, that property owes its origin mainly to the compulsion which is laid on men, as well as on other creatures, to defend themselves from each other and from the hostile forces of nature. At the very outset of his career, as presented to us in history, man appears to be relinquishing the hand-to-mouth life of the animal, and to be already armed with this instinct, which has raised about him the structure of modern civilisation. Each step in human progress has involved a further reliance on the industry which produces wealth, on the principle of property which protects it, and also a wider departure from the conditions which give to animals an uncertain survival in the struggle for existence.

The enormous gap which separates man from the lower animals is one of the principal difficulties in the theory of evolution. The difference is stupendous between the precarious life of the beasts that perish and the ease and certainty with which a civilised society obtains satisfaction of its daily wants. Yet how much of this depends on the familiar institution of property, and all that the term implies!

Let us next consider how this important condition of survival has been shared among the units which form organised and wealth-producing society. This may appear a cumbersome way of dressing up the familiar question, how wealth has been distributed among the men and women who create it. It enables us, however, to point out an analogy pregnant with meaning.

If we adopt the theory of evolution (and at the present time the lay public must bow to the almost unanimous opinion of scientific men), we must be struck by the fact that though the differentiation of species arises from the cumulative perpetuation of slight differences, yet throughout nature there exists among the members of the same species a large measure of equality. The powers, the instincts, and the important structural features which have enabled a species to survive, are common to the individuals of the species. The individuals who did not possess those powers, instincts, and features, were unfitted for survival and disappeared, and there remained species so clearly and distinctly defined, that for centuries the very idea of evolution and of intermediate varieties was inconceivable. The variations which in the course of biological time produce such stupendous results are in each generation infinitesimal, and only apparent to the very closest observation.

When we turn to man and view his relations to property, the most important condition of his survival, we find a totally different state of things. In most times and in most places property has been unequally divided.

The foregoing considerations appear to furnish

us with an hypothesis that if the ordinary course of evolution had proceeded without impediment, a more equal distribution of wealth might have been expected in human society. It is our object here to investigate and to explain what from our present point of view we may term this *unnatural* phenomenon of modern life.

One reason for this failure of nature to preserve her accustomed equality is very obvious. Among species of irrational beings in a state of nature, the weaklings and the stragglers perish. But man has, so to speak, put himself under his own domestication. Only in primitive society have famine, pestilence, and the other hostile forces of nature, been allowed free scope to gather the weeds from the human garden. In all civilised communities efficient steps have been taken to protect and to perpetuate the race of the unfittest. The unfittest, in the analogy which we are now following, are those who have not inherited, who cannot acquire, or who acquiring cannot keep enough to maintain themselves.

At this place we make no assumption that the laws of civilised society have been just and equitable. We are dealing with facts. It may be that the inheritance, acquisition, and keeping of property involve incidents which cannot be justified by religion or morality; but the truth remains that the unpropertied are those who, by reason of the superior strength of others or by reason of their own incompetence, have been unable to conform to the principal law of survival in civilised society.

In the natural course of events lower types have a tendency to disappear. In human society the existence of these lower types has been unnaturally prolonged. The life of the lowest stratum of our population would be just as precarious as the life of a savage, if it were not for the guarantee of maintenance given by our poor law. Below the savage the intermediate varieties have disappeared, and there is an enormous gap in the record of creation. Above the savage every single variety would seem to be preserved. Society at large will not allow any variety to die out, and it has thus perpetuated and extended by an artificial intervention forms of uneconomic existence which would otherwise have disappeared.

Society has felt itself obliged to provide for those who cannot provide for themselves, and it has done so without much apparent inconvenience. For in his struggle with nature man has been beyond measure successful. He has cleared all competitors from his path. The rest of nature is no longer a rival, but a minister to his wants. He can support a rapidly increasing population, and he is in a position to maintain, if he wishes to do so, an army of the unfittest. Mr. Darwin has based his theory of the origin of species on the fact that there is throughout nature a struggle for existence not only between different species, but between members of the same species. It is not too much to say that man has made all other species his ministers ; but the conflict still rages between the members of his own species ; and, as we have seen, philanthropy obliges him to provide for the unfittest that fall in the battle. This operation we may call the domestication of the unfittest by the fit. Now domestication has at its disposal valid forces for the production and preservation of new species and varieties, and if we pursue our argument to its logical conclusion, we may see reason to suspect that the 'unfit' are becoming specialised into a new parasitic variety of the human species, possessing different habits and different instincts to those which influence the rest of mankind. This action on the part of organised society springs from an instinct which is very deep-seated in the human mind. In its primitive aspect it is merely what we may call, for want of a better name, a gregarious instinct. This original and (if we may use the term without giving it any teleological significance) natural characteristic has been worked on by many forces which have arisen in the history of human progress. Religion and statecraft have seized upon it and turned it to many purposes. Nationality, philanthropy, centralised government, and socialism are all more or less manifestations of the same principle; and throughout the whole history of the world there is a perpetual struggle between the two principles of individualism and socialism.

Very early in the controversy the socialistic instinct set on men's necks a central government, which acted in a narrow class spirit, and devoted itself according to the lights of the time to preserving class distinctions and to making each class perform the duties which an ill-informed legislature thought necessary or important. No affair of life was too trivial to escape the direction of the central authority. This policy has bred disorder. Individuals, and even classes, have been excluded from gaining property; they have retained amid a growing civilisation the instincts of a savage condition. In the present day men have come to regard seriously the divorce of a portion of the masses from the blessings and advantages of civilisation. Thus the socialistic instinct which is itself responsible for the want of adjustment between property and numbers becomes imbued with a philanthropic zeal to repair the evils of its own creation. It is the business of the State, men argue, to make every one happy and to charge the cost on the rates. The older forms of state socialism were at least more logical. The State claimed the right of directing every act of the individual, he was bound to live in one place, to cultivate the land in one particular way, to follow such occupation and to wear such dress as the State thought right for him, and, as already said, no affair of life was too trivial to escape the direction of custom and authority. During long centuries the individual has contrived to disentangle himself from the trammels of collectivist authority. At the present day there is in certain quarters a reaction, and state socialism is again in the ascendant. In the old days of state interference the central authority was in the hands of a governing class. They in their wisdom formed some ideal of what a state should be, and proceeded to stretch the whole community to fit this procrustean bed of their own imagining. By laws against usury and regrating of provisions, by sumptuary regulations, by giving each man his place in the vast conception of the feudal system, the central authority based on custom and law dominated and controlled the conduct of the entire population.

At the present day the State is urged to revert again to philanthropic legislation, with a view of attaining a certain ideal. There is no disposition, however, to permit the same restraint on individual liberty. The State is to undertake a more difficult problem ; it may not coerce its citizens, but it is bound to make them happy, and to do so at the charges of the community at large.

In the old days there was some attempt made

by the central authority to control the rate at which individuals contracted responsibility. At present the only duty of the State is held to be the discharging of the responsibilities which have been incurred by the individual. Such, at least, is the argument of the socialistic dreamer. Individuals may spend their wages on the day they earn them, may marry when they please, may beget a horde of children, may be idle, imprudent, may spend their income in paying a voluntary tax—the State has been offered no right to control these proceedings; such a claim would be deemed an attempt to return to the foolish sumptuary legislation of mediæval times. The reactionary cry of the present day has not proceeded to this extreme. Therein it appears to be illogical. If out of individual liberty the State is asked to guarantee individual happiness, work for all who are willing to work, and purchasers for all that workers under such conditions can produce, education for all children that may be born, maintenance in sickness and old age for all who have made other use of their income, it is surely obvious that if it is to have any chance of fulfilling its guarantee it must also have the right to direct and control individual actions when these are engaged in creating responsibilities which they are under no obligation to discharge. It is a one-sided partnership, and one which is bound to result in insolvency, if individuals are to be free to create liability while society has only the burden of discharging the debt which others have incurred.

Returning from this digression to our analogy, it would appear that the unit of life, out of which all development and evolution proceeds, is an individual unit. It is this unit of an individual man which, in the process of evolution, has to get itself fitted to its environment. It is not possible to say that the socialistic or gregarious instinct is a weapon which individualism may not use. The individualist's ideal of anarchy *plus* the police constable does not entirely banish a centralised authority from human affairs. It is, however, clear that the socialistic instinct is only secondary in importance, and that it is only valuable when it is auxiliary to the use and comfort of individual life. It is easy to realise this as an academic proposition, but returning to the world we find that abstract ideas of society and government as something apart from the individuals who compose them, have been elevated by common consent into realities of far-reaching influence. The collectivist fictions thus created have undertaken duties which they could not perform, have been in turn philanthropic and tyrannical, and have introduced a wide-spread confusion into human affairs. Not only have they permitted the unfittest to survive, but they have actually created and perpetuated uneconomic varieties of human life

But as nature testifies, and as all breeders of domesticated animals know, there is a strong tendency, in any variety which is beginning to diverge, to cast back to an earlier type. This is especially so when there is no advantage or condition of survival attached to the variation in question, by nature or by the domesticator. In other words, species do not vary, in a permanent way, wantonly; but if the desire of a breeder, or a niche vacant in the economy of nature, supplies so to speak a demand for some variation of species, this variation by process of domestication or by the ordinary course of nature is almost certainly produced. We shall find this illustrated in human history. Society has seen fit to provide a maintenance for those who cannot support themselves. This fact is as effective for the production of a new variety as the whim of a breeder of stock. Christian sentiment requires that the strong shall not suffer the poor to perish of hunger. Further, it has been held to be one of the Christian virtues to give liberally to the maintenance of the poor, and no doubt it is so. Nevertheless the material conditions of the question have been too much overlooked. This care of the poor by the rich does not occur in the earliest stages of society. The unfit among savages die like the flies in winter. It is not till later that the well-to-do are themselves sufficiently secure to enable them to think of their less fortunate brethren.

When, however, society begins to maintain the poor at the direction of religion, the material laws which govern our destiny set two forces of divergence at work. On the one hand the possession of property gives rise to certain instincts. Deferred marriages, smaller families, closer calculation and more thrifty habits are all more characteristic of a propertied class than of a proletariate. The habits of a peasant proprietary is the oft quoted instance of this truth. The rich, therefore, grow richer in virtue of the greater reliance which they place on property as a condition of survival, for, according to all laws of evolutionary science, instincts grow stronger as they are exercised. Thus self-preservation by means of property becomes to the social life of man what the power of flight is to birds, the principal and most obvious item in its definition.

With the poor, although the main tendency is still upwards towards property and independence, there is a point at which an influence sets in in another direction. In this, and in most Christian countries, for centuries there has been a perfectly certain maintenance provided for the poor in virtue of their poverty. The State and the philanthropist guarantee support to the pauper. Endless Acts of Parliament have been passed, now to protect, now to coerce the poor, and as a consequence atrophy has settled down on some of the instincts which might otherwise have protected them. The first lessons in thrift, the first inducements to rely on property, the first motives to refrain from consuming wages on the day they are earned, arise from the desire of men to provide against the uncertainties of an unknown morrow, and for the inevitable period of sickness and old age. Our poor law and the ubiquitous philanthropist have done their best to prevent the poor man from the necessity of yielding to this desire. *Materially*, therefore, the moral teaching of the Church has created conditions which render possible the degradation of the poor. But the individualistic instinct is not so easily killed, and notwithstanding the snare, there is among the poor a latent, steady and withal effectual tendency to return to the true type of individual independence and self-assertion.

By using the term 'return,' we do not wish to imply that there is any golden age in the past. On the contrary, we conceive that progress has been continuous from the slavery of custom and superstition towards freedom of action and thought.

Progress has advanced by a reliance, often an unconscious reliance, on the principle of individual liberty. There have been periods of reaction, when this principle has been lost sight of. We are living in the midst of such a crisis at the present time. By the 'true type,' is meant the type which will give us more equality in our civilisation. This is the aim of all social reformers. Approximation to this true type can ultimately be gained only by permitting the individual to adjust himself to his environment. This adjustment cannot be made for him, all efforts in this direction have failed in the past, and have been, in fact, the cause of the modern conditions of inequality. Collectivist effort, without doubt, has conferred many benefits on mankind ; if there were no advantage in associated action, it could never have influenced human destiny with so compelling and far-reaching a force, but misuse of it has not been conducive to equality. It has helped to make a portion of mankind wealthy and powerful, but it has done so at the cost of individual development, and by a usurpation of the rights and claims of individual life.

In a word, collectivist effort, as embodied in the State, has become the master rather than the servant of the community which it governs. In the past the central power has been wielded in the narrow interest of classes. To-day modern sentiment would turn the State into a benevolent master, and urges it to make equality between all members of its household. Associated action, using the term in the widest sense, can produce more wealth than isolated action ; it can perhaps, if it so chooses, distribute this produce by some mechanical process which is intended to be equitable. Some men, however, rule their lives and conduct so that very little suffices for them. Others are less frugal. Some are extravagant in their appetites and requirements, and want besides a great deal for their children, and for their unprovided-for times of sickness and old age. Is the State to give to each man according to his requirements? In this case the richest and best-rewarded man is he who creates most liability.

These considerations bring us face to face with the ultimate impotence of benevolent state control, and force us back on the only alternative. Nature implants in each of her creatures a power of adjusting itself to varying conditions of life. The *use* of associated action is a characteristic of this latent power, but there must be no abdication of the individual instinct in favour of any instrument, however useful it may have been, if the true type of equal progress is to be preserved.

There is another aspect of the question which it is desirable to notice in this introductory chapter. If property has played this important part in uman development, and the fact is a truism that cannot be disputed, it is necessary to make some further analysis of its nature. The objects of human desire to which property attaches may, for our present purpose, and not with a view of making any scientific distinction, be divided into two classes :—

(1) Those commodities which do not require

to have further labour applied to them, which are in fact complete or ready for consumption and wear. These commodities represent the harvest of the world. They are constantly being consumed and worn out, and are replaced by others. Relatively to the whole wealth and resource of the world, the harvest even of many years is a very small quantity, and much the larger portion of those things to which property attaches will be found in our second division.

(2) This division consists of those objects of desire, on or about which labour must be bestowed before a finished product fit for consumption and use is made ready for the market. In this class we put the whole machinery of industry, the raw material and unfinished products of commerce, even the finished commodities which still require labour to transport them to the place where they are to be consumed. This portion of the world's wealth is in fact the potentiality which produces the harvest of the world, when suitable labour is applied to it. The possession of property in this class of wealth gives to its owner, not a finished commodity, but only a right and opportunity of labouring or employing labour to bring finished products into the market for consumption. For the wealth of a country does not consist in hoards of commodities which can be counted out and divided, but rather in a highly developed state of the resources of that

country, in its agriculture brought to a high state of efficiency by the science of farming, in productive mines, in its commerce and in its manufactures. All these would be valueless, and would not be subjects on which the instinct of property could be exercised, if it were not for the labour which has yet to be expended on them, and which is necessary before any harvest can be reaped. In this connection it has been pointed out by Mr. Mill that a hostile invasion, which for the moment appears to have crushed and destroyed the industry and wealth of an invaded country, after a short time leaves little trace of its passage, for the soil and most of the other opportunities of remunerative labour remain, and before long things have resumed their normal state.

It should further be noted that there is not an unlimited supply of such opportunities; if it were so they would cease to be valuable. Private property, as the universal expedient by which the distribution of valuable things has been effected, has attached therefore to these opportunities for labour. Private tenure is the alternative to a brute struggle for possession. Private tenure may be brought about by vesting ownership in the State instead of leaving the distribution to the laws of private property, but even the State cannot multiply these opportunities for remunerative labour. If it leases them out to individuals they will clamour for security of tenure, and the result will be the same. Value arises when many people want the same thing, and in whatever way the matter is arranged it is impossible for men to contract themselves out of this condition. It is inevitable, therefore, that the right to labour should be valuable, and therefore liable to attachment by the principle of private property.

If we are right then in attributing so much importance to this second division of property, it will follow that the greater part of a nation's wealth consists in a right and opportunity for remunerative labour. We now attempt to translate this into the language of the evolutionist, by saying that no man is fully equipped in the struggle for existence, who has not by means of property acquired either enough to keep him without labour, or an opportunity of labouring or hiring others to labour for him, at some one of the fountains of nature's bounty.

Enough has been said to indicate the hypothesis which these considerations appear to furnish. In the first place, it has been argued that property is a condition of man's survival, and that following the analogy of the rest of nature, we might have expected to see property somewhat equally divided. We have seen reason to think that man's own ingenuity has defeated the cruel, but in the end beneficent rules, under which the battle of life is fought in the world of nature. It was inevitable and right that humanity should mitigate the rigour of the struggle for existence. The question is, has the arrangement which human domestication has substituted for the law of nature worked well in all its details?

An analysis of the subject matter of property shows that most property conveys nothing but an opportunity of remunerative labour. This opportunity has of course a value in exchange. A. may sell his opportunities to B. or may lend them to him for a yearly rent or yearly interest, and, if he has enough of such opportunities, he may be able to live in idleness. This truth is clear enough with regard to land. If a man possesses a piece of agricultural land, it is plain that what he possesses is a right to use his spade or his plough, or if he so pleases, to sell or let the right to another. A man who possesses an 100*l.* worth of the productive enterprise of the country does not, it is true, possess always a right of employment, but in effect his investment does consist in the part ownership of an opportunity of labour for some one. Thus, the ownership of railway shares does not give their holders a right of being employed on the railway, but nevertheless a railway is nothing more than a highly developed opportunity for remunerative labour.

The fact that capital conveys little more than

a right of labour has fallen into oblivion, for except in countries where a peasant proprietary exists, the possession of capital and of land has as a rule passed away from the hands of the labourers who do the work thereon. In modern industry, which it should be remembered is not much more than 150 years old, capital and the right of labour which it gives has tended to centre in comparatively few hands. The owners of industrial property have been able to hire the labour of those who had no place of labour of their own. The fact, therefore, that property is in the main nothing more than a right to labour has been forgotten. Individuals or classes which possess no property conferring on them the right of remunerative labour, must be held, according to our analogy, to be unfitted. They are fitted for survival according to the rules of savage life, but they are unfitted according to the standard of civilised society. It may appear to be a paradoxical statement to say that the present division of society into a capitalist and labouring class is an unnatural phase of human domestication, and that it is opposed to all the analogies of natural evolution; we hope, however, in the course of this work to establish this proposition.

The increase of machinery, a fact of the utmost advantage to the majority of mankind, is at the present time very possibly operating with disastrous effect on the employment and happiness of large numbers of men whose labour it renders unnecessary. Surely this is a proof that man, during his period of domestication, has neglected some necessary precaution for keeping up reasonable relations between the different classes of industrial society. He has suffered a race of the unfittest to grow up, who have no interest in the improvement of national property by invention and machinery, who have none of the instincts which property engenders, and among whom the idea has been allowed to gain ground that the mere willingness to labour confers a right to employment and wages. The position now presented is a strange dilemma. A race of the unfittest has grown up, and is establishing its claim to be considered an incipient species. Either this process must continue till the parasitic variety destroys the healthy existence of the parent stock, or the unpropertied classes must be enabled in some way to acquire a share in the wealth of the country as a necessary condition in all healthy survival.

There are two ways of looking at this divorce between property and numbers which will constantly recur throughout this volume. The socialists see herein ground to attack the institution of private property, as far at least as it attaches to the productive apparatus of the world. This productive apparatus should be socialised, as they term it.

Our view, on the other hand, is that in these considerations we find a glorification and exaltation of the principle of private property. Numbers have been divorced from property which gives maintenance and opportunity for remunerative labour, and from the influence of property which makes for prudence and self-restraint. It is because classes have neglected or been deprived of this salutary provision, that our present case seems so unbearable. According to this view the collective or socialistic tenure of the productive apparatus of the world, although it might establish a short-lived mechanical equality of wealth or poverty, would yet deprive individual members of society of those instincts of prudence and calculation on which civilisation is founded. The most important of these is the instinct which regulates the rate of marriage, and consequently the rate of the increase of the population. It is an observed fact that the possession of private property, whether among the professional and well-to-do classes in England or among peasant proprietors abroad, supplies an operative and effective motive for checking the increase of population. We have no reason to suppose that a socialistic tenure of property would have the same effect. Indeed, if all men were placed in the position of workmen to whom a paternal government guaranteed employment, it is difficult to see where the virtue of prudence would come in. We shall have occasion very often to return to these conflicting views of human progress, and for the present we must leave them.

We have now stated our analogy, and indicated the hypothesis which we hope may guide us in our study of the history of English labour. Strange to say, there is much less difference of opinion about the facts of the case than might have been expected.

Our task now is to follow the divorce of labour and property, to ascertain the causes and results, to discover how far the present condition of things is inevitable and permanent, and if possible to throw a ray of light on some path that may be safe for the future.

CHAPTER II

THE SAME CONSIDERED HISTORICALLY. PRIMITIVE FORMS OF SOCIETY AND THE VILLAGE COMMUNITY

THE earliest organised form of human society of which we have any clear knowledge is the family. The theories of anthropologists with regard to primitive marriage and to stages of human history antecedent to the institution of the family are highly interesting and important, but they are much a matter of controversy, and they lie outside the purpose of our present enquiry. In a very early stage of man's history as a social being private property was already becoming a recognised institution.

Although the hunting grounds and the game which wandered there were of necessity common to all, yet the weapons of the chase were already tending to become the property of individual members of the family. The growing instinct to acquire property was first exercised upon objects which lay most convenient for appropriation, such as weapons, clothes, shelter. Each act of acquisition gained for the appropriator an advantage in the struggle for existence ; the act was repeated, the instinct became hereditary, the power of appropriation became a condition of survival. The necessity of private property has been pressed on man's attention by reason of the conditions by which he is surrounded. It was necessary, however, to create some sanction for this all-important principle. Human ingenuity has invented many explanations. The savage placed the property of his chief under the protection of the 'taboo.' The idea of private property, another authority tells us, was first recognised as between blood relations, and was religious in its origin. From another point of view we are told that might is right, and that the strong man armed keepeth his goods in peace. Jurists have pointed out the right of men to appropriate objects which are '*res nullius*.' Considerations such as these have played an important part in the development of the idea of property, and have combined to explain and sanction an already accomplished fact.

When men pass from a hunting to a pastoral stage of society, the same influences continue at work. Although at first cattle and sheep may have been common property, as soon as there ceased to be enough for all by reason of famine or some other disaster, the question arose, how is the common property of the tribe or family to be distributed? The strong, the ruling caste, will not consent to starve on an equality with their weaker neighbours. The process of the disintegration of the communistic tenure of movable chattels continues, and even at this stage the idea of private property in grazing land arose.

The reader will remember the story of the parting of Abraham and Lot. We are told 'Abram was rich in cattle and silver and gold, and Lot also which went with him had flocks, and herds, and tents. And the land was not able to bear them that they might dwell together. And there was a strife between the herdsmen of Abram's cattle and the herdsmen of Lot's cattle. And Abram said unto Lot, "Let there be no strife I pray thee between me and thee, for we be brethren. Is not the whole land before thee? Separate thyself, I pray thee, from me. If thou wilt take the left hand, then I will go to the right." . . Then Lot chose him all the plain of Jordan, and Lot journeyed east, and they separated themselves the one from the other.'

The next step in human development is the passage from the nomadic to the stationary agricultural state of society. And here at once it might have been thought was introduced a principle of disintegration which would immediately break up the system of holding land in common. For no man will sow where he has no security of reaping. The most obvious plan to follow was to allow men to appropriate for their own use portions of land, and to cultivate these according to their own fashion. But at this juncture of human history a very extraordinary phenomenon has everywhere taken place. From reasons which are perhaps inherent in the nature of the case, the process of appropriation which we have described as going on with regard to all movable property met with a check when it came to deal with land. Other objects of human desire had been appropriated by individuals, but when a portion of land came to be an object of desire, the power of individual appropriation seemed to fail. A counter-influence now made itself apparent, the power of the community as something having existence apart from the members who composed it, in other words the power of the State.

The family or the community of which the individual was a part now asserted, or had thrust on it, rights and duties in respect of land; and according to the best authorities all civilised society has passed through the stage of the village community. This fact, the causes which brought it about, and the results which follow from it, are in our understanding of the subject of such vast importance that it is necessary to consider in some little detail the nature of the village community.

This interesting form of society still survives

in India and in Russia, and it has been described by Sir H. Maine and Mr. Wallace in considerable detail. Mr. Seebohm and other writers have shown that it once was universal in England and in Germany. The close relationship of the institution in the various countries where it has been studied has been proved beyond a doubt by a great similarity of custom and system of cultivation. Occupancy within the limit of a village community of necessity conferred certain rights upon the occupier. It conferred a right to the use of the common waste, and to an allotment of the arable field. The system of common tillage was generally what is known as the three-field system, and it consisted in a very simple rotation of crops. A crop of wheat or rye was sown in the autumn and was reaped in the following autumn—the primitive harvesting operations were carried on late into the year. The next crop, of barley or oats, was sown in the early spring, and the third year the field lay fallow. In order that each household might have its share in each crop, a strip in each field was allotted to each, and so each man's land was scattered throughout the holding of the community. And, it is important to notice, these allotments were at first subject to periodical redistribution. The land belonged to the community, and it was administered according to custom by the patriarch or headman.

It is hardly necessary to point out how strong must have been the influence which set up and maintained a system of agriculture so highly inconvenient and unprofitable. Let us now consider in what that influence consisted.

Even at their first settlement on the land, the nomad tribes or families had an existence apart from the individuals who composed them. These groups were self-dependent, and in antagonism one to the other. They produced only for their own consumption. There was little occasion for trade, and such exchange and barter as passed between different tribes was often carried out at the boundary stone of the community or parish, in a semi-hostile fashion. Again, society was then in a constant state of intertribal war. Conquest still further increased the importance of the abstract community and the power of the headman who directed its affairs. The inhabitants of a conquered village were killed or made slaves, and their land was annexed. Fresh allotment of such land was made by the chief, and his authority and that of his little state naturally grew. In this way, parallel to the differentiation by means of property as between individuals, a similar differentiation was going on by the same process as between family and family or as between community and community. The community, in its struggle with other communities, appropriated the soil, as the individual did the movable property which lay to his hand. In this way, then, the process of individual appropriation was brought to a check by a new power, the power of the family, of the community, or, as we say in modern times, the power of the State. Thus in the first instance the appropriating unit with regard to land was the family or community, and not the individual.

It is not too much to describe this as a fact of stupendous importance, for here we witness the first encounter of opposing principles which are full of destiny for the human race. To make our meaning plainer, we must pass on to consider the results which have followed from this new principle of ownership. We have seen how the power of the abstract community, as represented in its headman, naturally grew. Gradually, and by a process sufficiently comprehensible, the ruler of the community came by the sheer force of custom to regard the land as his own, and, subject to the vested rights of occupiers, his claim was acquiesced in. It would hardly be correct to speak of this as an usurpation; it is rather a triumph of custom and legal fiction over the self-assertive instincts of individual life. A complete reversal of the original position had now taken place. The land was now considered to belong to the lord of the manor, subject to the rights of occupants and to the burden of maintaining its inhabitants, who now belong to the land and are regarded as *ascripti glebae*. The village community was, as Mr. Seebohm describes it, the shell in which a servile population existed. The lord was but the serf to whom custom had given a leading part. The subordination of the manorial lord to the superior lord, and of the superior to the king, is a well-known development of the feudal system. It appears to be the opinion of the best authorities that the progress from the village community to the feudal system has been continuous, and that there has been no violent transition. The advent of the later phases of feudalism was accelerated in England by the arrival of the Normans, but there is every reason to believe that no generic change was made. By a series of natural transitions one form of tenure passed into another. The village community, the Teutonic mark, the Roman benefice, the manor of Saxon and Norman times, are one and the same institution. Regarded from its ecclesiastical point of view the manor was the parish, an ominous name in the history of the poor.

Those persons whom the circumstances described had made the superiors in a stereotyped and customary system of land tenure, were marked out to be the rulers of the mediæval state. The remainder of the community sank into villenage. This is a point worth insisting on. We have attempted to show that the institution of property has been a principal condition in the survival of the human race, that progress on equitable and safe lines can only be made by giving to the fullest extent scope to the individual instinct of self-preservation which prompts each man to acquire property. A system which checks this, which establishes inequality and shuts out from the enjoyment and education of property a class of the population, is full of danger to the common weal. The first interference with the appropriating power of the individual has by a natural train of causation given us the feudal system and all the inequalities of a landed aristocracy. Property has thus played an important part in determining the form, not only of our social arrangements, but also of our political government. Manorial rights and the property connected with them were thrown, as we have seen, into the hands of a limited class. Thus a landed aristocracy was created, which was for centuries to form the ruling caste in European society. Sir H. Maine has acutely pointed out that a governing class or aristocracy has always been based on the possession of property. Prowess in the field of battle was only one of the many ways to acquire the favour of the king, and to receive a reward in land and vassals. The modern idea which opposes aristocracy to wealth can claim no justification in the record of history.

If, then, we are correct in regarding these facts as the result of the first conflict between the opposing interests of the individual and the State, we shall conclude that the feudal system is nothing more or less than the failure of an attempt to hold land on a socialistic tenure. It is difficult to use language which does not give a modern and inappropriate colouring to these incidents. Ideas of abstract justice, it need hardly be said, are quite foreign to the mind of primitive societies, and ethical considerations have little or nothing to do with the early history of property. In modern days the ethical, philanthropic, socialistic instinct prompts men to use the central authority to attain objects which appear to them to be desirable. In primitive times the same instinct, which for want of a better term we have called gregarious, seized on the land as being the principal factor for securing maintenance and wealth. The objects to which society was then striving were objects which to us are neither desirable nor interesting, and we presume a later age will say the same of our ideals. The socialistic purpose of feudal communities was to make property subservient to the feudal ideal, to make and to maintain a military system, of which the king was the head. A definite place in a complete system was given to each class of baron, tenant, serf, and cottager, who had dwelling room in the land. It was a system of socialism more thorough than anything which has even been imagined by modern enthusiasts.

The division of England into manors must be dated back into prehistoric times. Just as the custom and rule of the manor had established its ascendency over the inhabitants who lived within its limits, so an analogous process of warfare went on between the central or imperial authority and the jurisdiction of the manorial courts. The point has been set out with much force by Mr. Denton in his 'History of the Fifteenth Century':—

> Long before Parliament met at Westminster and imposed taxes and assisted in making laws for the whole kingdom, the most important functions of such a parliament were performed by the manorial courts throughout England. . . . It was not without remonstrance on the part of suitors in these local courts, that Parliament and the king's courts claimed after a time to pass laws affecting manorial rights, and to adjudicate on matters touching the tenure of land and the customs of manors.

The great work of Edward I. was to increase the power of the king's courts and of the central government. The strong hand of the king and of his successors prevailed, and the lawyers invented a sanction for the procedure. 'It is a *fiction* of our English tenures,' says Blackstone, 'that the king is the universal lord and original proprietor of all the lands in his kingdom.' Mr. Denton quotes authority for the following dictum: 'Our law admits not anything, either real or personal, to go *primo occupanti*; but where an owner cannot be found the common law gives it to the king.'[1] This claim has its analogy in the custom of the manor, when the estates even of *libere tenentes*, on failure of heirs, escheated to the lord. The imperial central authority in course of time swallowed up and destroyed the manorial court. At the present day the shuttlecock is sent flying back in the other direction. Decentralisation, devolution of the duties of the imperial parliament to the county councils, is the fashion of the hour. It is to be feared that the further necessary devolution of administration from all centralised government in favour of individual liberty, is no part of the creed of the modern politician.

The land of England, then, was held on a very complete system of service tenures. The distinction between the so-called free tenants and those who, in name as well as reality, were serfs, seems to have been more apparent than real, for even the free tenants were dependent on their superior lord. Their freedom consisted only in the fact that they had commuted their labour service and acquired the right of using their own labour; politically they still were under the control of the manorial system; and many of the incidents of their tenure were of a servile origin. The nearest approach to complete private property in land is to be found in the grants of 'boc land' made to the religious houses out of the folkland. Individuals appear to

[1] Callis' *Reading on Sewers*, p. 45.

have been enabled to make colonies on the waste, and this class occupied a place next in importance to the free tenants. Again, there was the class known as cotters, who occupied small holdings, and the serfs, who also held small farms, both on an entirely servile tenure.

The land controlled by the lord of the manor was divided into the domain and the waste. His domain was cultivated by the servile labour of his tenants, who, in return for these services rendered to the ruling power, had their own allotments in the arable fields, and their rights in respect of the waste. When their due service was rendered, they were entitled to work for themselves. The inequalities established under this form of land tenure were increased and confirmed by other causes of similar origin. The political system became based essentially on the landed interest, and on the vassals and power which this bestowed.

It was therefore necessary for its preservation to maintain intact the lordships which supported it. A subdivision of property and of the rights and power of property would have destroyed the privilege of the ruling caste, and would have impaired the efficiency of military feudalism. Primogeniture therefore, from this point of view, became under the feudal system a convenient and useful custom. But the younger sons of the ruling caste must be provided for, and the whole framework of society accommodated itself to this purpose. The foreign wars of our early Norman kings, the administration of the power and revenues of the Church, afforded employment for the younger branches of noble families. Sinecures were invented, oppressive monopolies were granted, and official posts with handsome salaries and perquisites were created. Thus the power of the nobility was strengthened and consolidated, and provision was made for the disinherited at the expense of the productive industry of the country.

Again, the poorer free tenants found their position in many cases less eligible than that of slaves. The chronicler, Roger of Hoveden, tells us that when William I. devastated Northumbria, so great was the famine and misery that men were forced to sell themselves into slavery. The insecurity both of life and property made men wish to attach themselves to the fortune of some powerful protector, and free tenants not unfrequently made over the land to some neighbouring lord, 'in commendation.' In return for this, the lord admitted the donor as his tenant, and agreed to give him the protection of the manor.

In this brief outline we have not attempted to enter into any of the interesting controversies which concern themselves with the extent of the freedom enjoyed by the members of the Teutonic mark, and how far this freedom was eclipsed in the early development of English land tenure. In the necessarily imperfect account given of the genesis of the feudal system, and of the ruling caste which it maintained, one important fact is to be noted, namely, that when our country emerged into the light of historical times, a large proportion of its rural population held land on a tenure which in many respects was of a servile nature.

The history of mediæval England, which follows on the period now described, is the history of the disentanglement of the individual from the trammels of serfdom and servile tenure. Amid what may fairly be described as an universal conspiracy to exalt the State and the classes in whose interest the State was administered at the expense of individual property and right, we shall witness an extraordinary power of self-assertion and recuperation as being still at the service of the individual.

Naturam expellas furcâ, tamen usque recurret.

We shall see, too, how this attempt of the individual to reassert his position has been frustrated, and how a false step once taken brings with it a long train of evils.

Human progress is a matter about which it is idle to be impatient. We cannot hope for regeneration in the course of a lifetime. Rather we must regard man's development in society as a portion of the evolution of the world, and make bold to ask for its consummation a period of almost geological time.

CHAPTER III

ENGLISH VILLENAGE

It would be presumptuous in one who is not a specialist to attempt any new reading of English history. Happily, in the subject now under consideration, there is a very general agreement as to facts. The difficulty lies in the interpretation of these facts. Some consensus of opinion has described the fifteenth century as the golden age of the English labourer. One is naturally inclined to distrust the glowing pictures of a prosperous past, which are too often drawn by pessimists as a ground for the disparagement of their own times. The golden age of such writers is too often found to be a mere *ignis fatuus*, which vanishes when we attempt to examine it at close quarters. Indeed, there is nothing about which men differ more than in an attempt to estimate the amount of prosperity which exists in any given community. This is a subject about which contemporaries cannot agree. Everyone who has considered the question must feel that, when attempting to gauge the happiness of bygone generations, he is dealing with facts which are very ill ascertained and very liable to error.

There is no need to dispute the characteristics which have been ascribed to the position of the labourer in the fifteenth century. The statement must, however, be considered relatively to the position of the rest of the population. It is very possible that the condition of the labourer approached nearer to the condition of the higher classes than at any other period of history. Mr. Thorold Rogers describes the time as one of rude plenty. It would be right, if we desire to understand the position, to accentuate the rudeness as well as the plenty. When we reflect on the famines, the plagues, the skin diseases, the miserable quality of the food, the insecurity of life and property, the hovels in which the people lived, and the tyranny and oppression of a time of unsettled government, we shall probably think more of the rudeness and barbarism of the whole nation than of the alleged plenty enjoyed by the poor.

Leading up to this period of alleged prosperity, our enquiry will follow in chronological order the development of the manorial system, whose origin we have stated in the last chapter.

For many centuries agriculture and the trades connected with it were the principal, if not the only, industries in England, and as a starting-point we cannot do better than reproduce the picture of an

English manor in the thirteenth century as it is drawn by Professor Rogers in his valuable work, 'Six Centuries of Work and Wages.'

The manor selected is the manor of Cuxham, in Oxfordshire. At the close of the thirteenth century this was the property of Merton College, Oxford, and by good fortune there still exists considerable documentary evidence of the dealings of the lords of the manor with their tenants. The account may be taken as a representative description of an English village for the first fifty years of the fourteenth century. First, then, there was the lord to whom the manor house and the demesne belonged. On the other hand, were the tenants or occupiers of land within the limit of the manor. These last occupied their holdings on very various tenures.

Under the lords of the manor, *i.e.* the warden and scholars of Merton College, the two principal tenants were bound to render certain military services in circumstances and under conditions more or less clearly understood and defined. These services were either commuted or commutable into a 'scutage,' or fixed yearly payment. Next there was a free tenant who held $3\frac{3}{4}$ acres of land, the portion of his wife, at a rent of 3*s*. a year. He besides had a messuage of 9 acres for which he paid 1 lb. of pepper, at Mr. Rogers' valuation about 1*s*. 6*d*. The rector of the parish held a part of the common arable field, for which he paid 2*d*. a year.

The prior of a neighbouring monastery had a messuage on condition of offering prayer for the soul of the donor. The miller paid a rent of 40*s.* a year, and the tenants were bound to bring their corn to his mill. Another tenant had a cottage, for which he had to supply two lights in the church. The rest of the population were serfs (*nativi*), or cottagers (*cotterelli*). On the estate there were 13 families of the first and 8 of the second class. Each serf had a holding of not less than 12 acres of arable land, his rent was paid almost entirely in kind and in labour, of which the following are the principal items. He paid ½*d.* on November 12, and 1*d.* whenever he brewed. He had to supply a quarter of wheat seed at Michaelmas; a peck of wheat, 4 bushels of oats, and 3 hens on November 12; at Christmas a cock and 2 hens and two pennyworth of bread. He had to plough, sow, and till half an acre of the lord's land, as directed by the bailiff. He had also to reap for the lord three days, with one man hired at his own charges. Mr. Rogers estimates these payments and services at 9*s.*, of which 3*s.* must be allowed for house rent. Thus the rent of 12 acres of land was at the rate of 6*d.* per acre. Some of the serfs appear to have held other lands, for which they paid in labour about 2*s.* 4*d.*

The cottagers held little more than a tenement with a small piece of ground attached, for which they paid rent from 1*s.* 2*d.* to 2*s.* per annum. They were bound in addition to harvest and haywork, and in some instances to help in the washing and shearing of sheep. At other times they were free labourers, or possibly craftsmen. The number of cottagers, comparatively to the serfs and other occupying tenants, appears to have been small both in Cuxham and in the other manors mentioned by Mr. Rogers. The cottagers, however, like the serfs, occupied a definite position on the land. A thirteenth century village contained, says Mr. Rogers, from 60 to 70 inhabitants. The Cuxham village must have been somewhat larger. The modern area of the manor is 487 acres. The lord of the manor cultivated 181½ acres, he held perhaps about 60 more in fallow, in all about 240. The serfs held about 170 acres, and other tenements accounted for perhaps 30 acres. Thus 440 acres out of 487 were under occupation, leaving only some 40 or 50 acres as common pasturage. Mr. Rogers, however, conjectures that this conclusion may be erroneous, and that the ancient boundaries probably left a much larger area of common land.

The lord of the manor by means of servile labour cultivated, as we have seen, 181½ acres. He was not always resident; in the particular case of Cuxham, the college employed one of the serfs as bailiff, and the office descended from father to son for several generations, in fact till the family were cut off in the great plague in 1348. Sometimes, though rarely at this period, the lord let his domain, but in all such instances the farm was let with the stock on it. Practically, such a tenant was rather a bailiff than a farmer cultivating on his own account. At the end of the tenancy the stock had to be accounted for, and returned intact to the landlord. The capital was entirely supplied by the lord, and not by the tenant.

The serf was in every way bound to the soil; he could not leave to become a soldier or a priest, nor could he engage in trade or sell his cattle, without the leave of his lord. His domestic arrangements, even the marriage of his daughters, were under the control of his superior, and fines had to be paid on all the important transactions of his life. On the other hand he was a peasant proprietor, holding his land on a fixed rent, on conditions that were not onerous, though highly inconvenient and arbitrary. By the middle of the fourteenth century the labour rents had been very generally commuted into fixed money payments.

With the higher class of tenant the process of commutation had begun even earlier. During the French wars of our early kings, the military tenants of the Crown found it inconvenient to leave their homes for foreign lands, and they became anxious to commute their services for a money payment or scutage. Such an arrangement was welcome to an impecunious king, to whom a fixed revenue was even more valuable than a supply of fighting men. The same process went on with regard to the serf on the manor. In the earliest work on English husbandry, written probably about 1249, Walter de Henley dwells on the great difficulty experienced by the lord of the manor in exacting a due and diligent performance of the labour rent. It is very obvious that forced labour must always have been carried out in a very perfunctory manner. It is not, therefore, surprising that the manorial lords were willing to commute the labour due from their serfs into a fixed money payment. The tenants, on their part, were not averse to escape from the troublesome and ill-defined obligations under which they lay for a clear and explicit agreement to pay a fixed yearly rent.

It will be observed that, except the miller, there does not appear to have been any tradesman or artisan living within the manor of Cuxham. The village mill was a valuable monopoly for which the lord received a handsome rent, but with this exception the subdivision of labour, as we understand it in modern times, was unknown. There were, of course, smiths, masons, and other domestic craftsmen scattered about in English villages, but in all probability they employed a considerable portion of their time on the land, either on their own holding or on those of their neighbours. Further, beyond their own tools, they kept no stock of the materials of their trade. The capitalist tradesman had not yet arisen. The raw material, the metal, the stones and mortar, the wood and other necessaries, were supplied by the lord or farmer who had occasion for the services of the artisan. In other respects, also, the English agricultural home of the period was self-contained. Coarse linen and woollen material was manufactured at home by the women of the family. It is true that a considerable wool-spinning and weaving trade was springing up in Norfolk, and later in the south-west of England ; but the chief encouragement of this trade came not from English homesteads, but from the Flemish merchants who traded with the court and with the continent.

As already pointed out, the greater part of the population of England was attached to the soil, and derived its maintenance from agriculture. Nor is this a mere statement of an economic fact ; it was actually the law of the land. By a law of Athelstane (924) it was ordained 'that lordless men of whom no law can be got, the kindred be commanded that they domicile him to folkright and find him a lord in the folkmote.' This law gives the keynote of what may be called the early poor law and police legislation of our country. For the legislation in question had two objects in view, and for its purpose it sought to sanction by legal enactment the customs handed down from the primitive economy of the village community. On the one hand it decreed that every man should have a settlement in some manor or parish, and on the other hand that every manor or parish should be responsible for the conduct and good behaviour of its inhabitants. The subordination of all men to parochial, or, to speak more correctly at this date, to manorial jurisdiction, was a perquisite or right of the lord of the manor. At the same time it also conferred on all men a right to attach themselves to the land of some particular manor. These two principles run through and explain most of the early legislation on the subject. On one side the law is always seeking to bring back vagabonds and lawless men to the servitude of some lord. Against this the duty of the manor to be surety for the behaviour of those within its limits was clearly enacted. The humanitarian aspect of the poor law is of later date. The legislature of this time was wholly unable to protect industrious and comparatively wealthy persons in the enjoyment of their property. The hands of the government, itself often the greatest of marauders, were too full to allow it to think of the interests of the poor. Henry II. was an able and powerful ruler, but a description of his royal progresses reads like the account of 'processions of organised mobs perambulating the country, and levying contributions without stint or mercy upon all who unhappily came within their reach.' When this was the conduct of the highest feudal authority in the land, it is hardly necessary to point out that respect for human life and property was not likely to be observed by the lower barons, in whose hands the local government of the country rested. There are numerous enactments against robbery and vagabondage, imposing barbarous penalties and mutilations to be inflicted on those who were found guilty of such offences. Many of them, notably the Statute of Winchester (13 Edward I., 1285), attempt to fix the responsibility for misconduct on the district which harbours the offenders: and, as already pointed out, 'the most ancient statutes for regulating the poor were enacted to repress vagrancy, not to provide for their maintenance.'

Such being the condition of the rural population, a word must now be said on the life of the town population of the period. There is, however, very little to be told. The occupations of the town did not differ much from those of the country. The towns were merely villages, and the great cities, which were in after ages to be the home of a teeming population, did not exist. The beginnings of trade were gathering in the towns protected by charter, or round the walls of great monasteries, but it was the trade of the merchant rather than that of the manufacturer. Manufacture was carried on in the home and by the hand. The trade of the towns, except the export of wool and occasionally of grain, both depending on the activity of the country industry, was confined to the humbler domestic industries, and these on a very limited scale. Considerable numbers of serving men were retained in the trains of the great nobles and ecclesiastics and in the service of the monasteries and religious houses. The great insecurity of life and property hindered the material progress of the country. The surplus wealth was expended in civil and foreign war, and though all lived in a state of rude plenty, arts and manufactures were neglected. The towns, in fact, were merely the markets where the country produce was sold, and their business was entirely auxiliary to the business of the country. The Government, both local and imperial, was always in search of sources of taxation, either for the legitimate purposes of revenue, or more often with a design of enriching a royal favourite. It began, therefore, to grant to towns which were willing to pay for them, charters and monopolies both of market and manufacture. Considerable antagonism between the town and the country in time arose from this fact. The towns attempted to put restrictions on the operations of the rural industries and to establish separate interests of their own, which proved in time to be very burdensome to the interest of the country at large. On the whole, however, it was not till a later date that the English towns began to exercise an important influence on the economy of the English industrial classes.

This state of things continued in force till about the middle of the fourteenth century. The characteristic event of the period was the gradual emancipation of a servile population, which was slowly but surely acquiring the position of a peasant proprietary. Mr. Hallam, after describing the degraded position of the servile tenants, proceeds as follows:

> From so disadvantageous a condition as this of villenage, it may cause some surprise that the peasantry of England should ever have emerged. The law incapacitating a villein from acquiring property placed, one would imagine, an insurmountable barrier in the way of his enfranchisement. It followed from thence, and is positively said by Glanvil, that a villein could not buy his freedom because the price he tendered would already belong to his lord. And even in the case of free tenants in villenage it is not easy to comprehend how their uncertain and unbounded services could ever pass into slight pecuniary commutations, much less how they could come to maintain themselves in their lands, and mock the lord with a nominal tenure according to the custom of the manor.[1]

The explanation of this phenomenon will involve us, says the same authority, in a very obscure enquiry. The genuine history of mankind

[1] Hallam, *Middle Ages*, iii. 257, *sq.*

has been passed over with slight and partial notice by contemporary writers ; and our most patient industry can hardly at present put together enough of the fragments to suggest a tolerably clear representation of ancient manners and social life.

If we take what may be considered as the simplest case, that of a manor divided into demesne lands of the lord's occupation and those in the tenure of his villeins, performing all the services of agriculture for him, it is obvious that his interest was to maintain just so many of these as his estate required for its cultivation.

In course of time, as alienation of parts of the manor took place, the lord required a smaller amount of labour on his land.

The purchasers under these alienations had occasion for labourers ; and these would be free servants in respect of such employers, though in villenage to their original lord . . . . so these became hired labourers in husbandry for the greater part of the year. This perhaps was the origin of the free labourer. Some of the more fortunate villeins crept into property as well as freedom under the name of copyholders.

Copyhold lands (says Mr. J. Williams, 'Real Property,' p. 336) are lands holden by copy of court roll, that is, the muniments of the title to such lands are copies of the roll or book in which an account is kept of the proceedings in the court of the manor to which the lands belong. For all copyhold lands belong to, and are parcel of some manor. The rise of the copyholder from a state of uncertainty to certainty of tenure appears to have been very gradual. Britten, who wrote in the reign of Edward I., describes villeins as persons who might be ousted from their tenements at the will of their lord. In the reign of Edward III., however, the entry of a lord on his copyholder was adjudged lawful, '*because he did not do his services*, by which he broke the custom of the manor,' which seems to show that the lord could not at that time have ejected his tenant without cause. In the reign of Edward IV. the judges gave to copyholders a certainty of tenure, so long as they perform the duties which the custom of the manor requires. Hallam mentions another cause which contributed to form a class of hired labourers, namely, the facility with which villeins were able to escape from the place of their servitude. The law favoured the fugitive villein, and residence for a year in a walled town or borough barred the claim of the lord. By such means, concludes Mr. Hallam, a large proportion of the peasantry before the middle of the fourteenth century had become hired labourers instead of villeins.

A very similar view is taken by the Bishop of Chester.[1] The history of the villein class in early Norman times is very obscure. His position had suffered under the stringent and more developed system of feudalism introduced by the Normans. In Anglo-Saxon times his estate was one of de-

[1] Stubbs's *Constitutional History*, i. 427.

pression, but not of helplessness. The distinctions among the lower class of tenants are far more minute than can be recognised at the present day. There were, according to the authority of Doomsday Book, 25,000 servi, who must correspond, says the Bishop, to landless labourers, 82,000 bordarii, and 7,000 cotarii, classes which are not very distinct the one from the other, and 110,000 villani; above these came the liberi homines and the socmanni. The tendency of law and social habit was to throw into one class of native or born villeins the whole of the population described as servi, bordarii, and villani. He quotes an entry in a document of the time of Henry I., in which the classes named are treated as part of the stock on an estate. The servus is said to have disappeared early and to have been merged in the semi-servile class of the villani. The Church made it a merit in a lord to grant manumission to his villeins, 'but it by no means follows that manumission was a benefit, if thereby the newly-enfranchised lost his claim to be maintained on the lord's land and must forthwith look for new service or throw himself on the chances of war or trade.'

These causes no doubt were leading to the establishment of a labouring class who were not paid, as were the ordinary peasantry, by a grant of land. The landless labourer was a free man, he had lost his hold on the land but had gained his freedom; others were more fortunate, and in order to explain the process of their emancipation, where the facts are so obscure, we are tempted to rely on the natural probability of the case, and to lay emphasis on the words of Mr. Hallam, that many at this period crept into property as well as freedom under the name of copyholders, and thus to attribute the enfranchisement which, all agree, was taking place, to the natural self-assertion of individual life. At this juncture, namely, at the middle of the fourteenth century, an event occurred which precipitated the change, and, for the moment, entirely altered the aspect of the situation.

CHAPTER IV

THE BLACK DEATH AND THE DIVORCE OF THE LABOURER FROM THE LAND

THE most probable estimate of the population at the beginning of the fourteenth century, gives the number at about 2,350,000.[1] For many reasons it appears likely that population was not at this date increasing at a very rapid rate. Famines, notably those of 1315 and 1321, the absence of sanitary and medical skill, and the insecurity of life must all have tended to keep down the increase of numbers. It is, moreover, an observed fact that, among a peasant proprietary, population does not increase faster than the sustenance which has to support it. It is difficult to estimate what power of expansion there may have been through reclamation of waste land; there is no evidence, however, that agricultural skill was at all progressive. Root crops and grasses were entirely unknown. These, in fact, were not introduced into England till the seventeenth century. While agriculture rested under the disadvantage

[1] McCulloch, *Account of British Empire*, i. 396.

of the most primitive form of the common field system, it is not likely that increasing wealth offered much encouragement to an increase of population. There is no evidence, in fine, that anything in the nature of over-population existed at the time.

In 1348-1349, at a period when the numbers of the people were by no means excessive, the country was visited by the terrible calamity of the Black Death. Various computations are given of the mortality that ensued. Estimates, accepted by the gravest modern historians, declare that from one-third to one-half of the whole population perished. Contemporary historians place the mortality at nine-tenths of the whole population. This extraordinary misfortune threw the entire rural economy of England into confusion. The unprecedented mortality established a labour famine. Royal proclamations were issued, stringent acts of parliament were passed, to compel labourers to work at the old rate of wages. Neither proclamation nor acts were of much avail. A great increase of wages at once took place, and without doubt the prospects and condition of the labourer for hire were greatly improved. Mr. Rogers calculates that in the period between 1350-1400, the rise in agricultural wages was from 40 per cent. to 70 per cent. at the very least. It was probably more. At harvest time it amounted to treble the former rate. The wages of women were doubled or even trebled. The value of artisan labour rose from 50 per cent. to 90 per cent. At the same time there was no rise in the price of agricultural produce, which would oblige the labourer to spend more in the purchase of his daily bread. Rent fell in many instances to one-third of its former amount. In a word, the labourer became the master of the situation..

It is generally assumed that the disaster of the Black Death ensured the triumph of labour, and prepared the way for the alleged prosperity of the following century. The advantage which the catastrophe gave to the hired labourer is indubitable, but there appear to be some larger questions involved. It must be remembered that the prosperity of the country at this period rested on the wide distribution of ownership in the principal factor of production, namely land. Further, there were two alternatives by which the villein or unfree labourer could creep into property and freedom: one, by eluding his servitude and becoming a free labourer away from the place where his service was due; the other, by clinging to his land and gradually commuting his labour rent for the safer and more definite tenure of copyhold. The extraordinary and fictitious value given to hired labour, by reason of the sudden decimation of the population, gave a strong impulse to the first of these alternatives. The equilibrium of healthy progress was disturbed, and encouragement was given to the formation of the agricultural labouring class. A further step was taken in the divorce of classes from property. It is true that for long the evil results of this did not show themselves. Down to the end of the fifteenth century wages remained high, and, as already stated, this century is often termed the golden age of the English labourer; but we cannot regard as favourable to the best interests of our country a train of circumstances which separated from the rest of society a labouring caste. At this juncture of history it was the fate of the agricultural labourer to relinquish, for the sake of a momentary advantage, his hold upon the land. Henceforward the landless class grew and multiplied with alarming rapidity. The course of events had deprived them of a share in the principal productive factor, and they lost or never acquired the instincts of prudence and self-restraint which have always dominated the domestic economy of a peasant proprietary. Acquisition of property, by means of thrift and careful husbandry, as a possible course of conduct faded from the horizon of the labourer's hope. He became content to live and multiply on the maintenance provided by wagedom. For the time employment was plentiful, and his reliance thereon seemed to be justified; but when population had attained to its old limit the fallacious character of this reliance became apparent. A consideration of what might have been is seldom profitable, but with a view of making our meaning clear, it is suggested that if the orderly development of society had been suffered to continue, the individual would have gradually become disentangled from the trammels of feudalism, and have crept into property and freedom under the name of copyholder. Thus the institution of the agricultural labouring caste might have been averted, and the whole history of industry might have been different. But such speculation is idle. It is freely admitted that the sudden enhancement of the value of labour was not the only cause capable of producing the result described. The same condition might have been brought about by a totally different chain of circumstances, as indeed has happened in other countries.

To complete our picture of the effect of the Black Death, we have yet to consider the change which it occasioned in the condition of the landlords and larger farmers. Their position was indeed very serious. They were obliged to pay higher wages and higher prices for those manufactured articles in which wages were a large element of cost, but they received the old low rates for agricultural produce. What was to be done? If they were unable to secure labour at more reasonable rates, the profit of their industry was gone. To escape from this difficulty they invoked the power of the State, which was ruled by members of their own class. An attempt was made to return to the old system of forced labour. Tenants had very generally commuted their labour rent, and would only labour at the new scale of high wages. The law of the land was called into action to revoke the contract and to enable the lord to extract the old labour dues from his semi-enfranchised tenantry. It is worthy of note that the enactments of the famous Statute of Labourers, which was passed immediately after the year of the Black Death, were directed as much to forcing people to labour as to regulating the rate of wages. It was ordered in this important statute that no labourer shall decline to labour at the customary wages of 1347, that is, of the year before the plague. Labourers are not to quit service on pain of imprisonment. The manor court, the court in which the influence of the manorial lord was supreme, was charged with the enforcement of these regulations. Artisans were made liable to the same or similar conditions. Alms were not to be given to able-bodied persons. Lords of manors were forbidden to pay more than the customary rate of wages. Wages so paid were liable to confiscation to the king. Food was to be sold at reasonable prices. The Act may be described as an attempt to regulate the confusion which arose from the labour famine caused by the Black Death. The preamble of the Act sets out the scarcity of servants, who seeing their masters' necessity will not serve unless they receive excessive wages, and states that many prefer to beg rather than work for lower wages. In the spirit of the old legislation it is ordered that every man who has no proper land of his own, nor having of his own whereof he may live, shall be bound to serve him, which him shall require and take only the wages accustomed to be given in the places where he oweth to serve. Workmen in towns are prohibited from going out in summer 'if they may serve in the same town.' An exception is made in favour of harvesting labourers from the counties of Stafford, Lancaster, and Derby, the people of Craven and from the marches of Wales and Scotland, who may go and come in safety as *heretofore.* This last provision affords evidence that even in earlier times the rural population in the grain-growing country was not sufficient for the harvest. A similar Act was passed two years later, and may be regarded as a proof of the inoperativeness of the Statute of Labourers, for all these regulations were of little avail, and the law was evaded in every possible way. Mr. Rogers points out a very curious instance of this, which occurs in the account of the bailiff of Cuxham rendered to Merton College. Entries are made of payment of labourers for threshing wheat at 5*d.* per day. The entry is then corrected and 3*d.* substituted, and similar corrections occur throughout the account. Mr. Rogers suggests that this device was adopted for the purpose of evading the Statute of Labourers.

But the landlord interest did not give way without a struggle. Although direct legal enactment proved of no avail, a continuous attempt was made to enforce the expiring system of servile labour. This appears to be the explanation of the rebellion of Wat Tyler in 1381. The popular account, which attributes the outbreak to an insult offered to Tyler's daughter by one of the tax-gatherers, will hardly explain the wide-spread and apparently organised rising which took place.

The object of the rebellion was to obtain the formal abolition of servitude. The insurgents demanded abolition of slavery for themselves and for their children, low rents, and the right to buy and sell in all fairs and markets. The incidents of the struggle are well-known. The king yielded to the demand of the rebels, but when the concession was reported to Parliament, the reply was—

> That all grants of liberties and manumission to the said villeins and bond tenants obtained by force are in disherison of them the Lords and Commons, and to the destruction of the realm and therefore null and void, their consent thereto they would never give to save themselves from perishing all in one day.

The protest of the Lords and Commons was quite unable to stem the stream. High wages continued to be paid, and the tenants succeeded in making good their claim to freedom.

To save themselves from ruin and to turn their land to some valuable purpose, the landlords were obliged to look round for other and less objectionable expedients. The first plan resorted to by the landlord seems to have been a change in his plan of farming. Up to this time he had cultivated his land himself by means of servile or hired labour. When this system could no longer be carried on profitably, owing to the emancipation of their serfs and the high rate of wages, it became customary for the landlord to let his land with the stock on it to a farmer, or, if the estate was a large one, to more than one farmer. The tenant with his family did the greater part of the work, and could manage more economically than a landlord who was dependent on a bailiff for supervision.

Some of the accounts kept under this form of lease have been examined by Mr. Rogers.

It appears that a balance-sheet was made out at the end of each year. The tenant was obliged to keep up the tale of the stock which belonged to the landlord. Over and above this the landlord received a rent, and the tenant made as much profit as he could out of the transactions of the year. Under such conditions the tenants were not capitalists; but if their farming was profitable, they soon saved money, and by purchase of stock on their own account the form of lease changed very naturally into something like its present form. Such an event was not unimportant in preparing the way for a new order of things. According to the computation of Mr. Rogers, land rented at 6*d.* an acre was worth about twelve to sixteen years' purchase, that is to say from 6*s.* to 8*s.* per acre. The stock upon it, at the lowest computation, must have been worth from 16*s.* to 20*s.* per acre. Under the old system, when both stock and land belonged to the same person, the landowner must have had more personal than real property, and although the custom of primogeniture was universal as regards land, he was still able to make provision for his younger children without burdening his land. Under the new system, landlords who did not cultivate their own land had not of necessity any personal property, out of which legacies could be given to younger children. The difficulty was met to some extent by the absorption of younger sons into the ranks of the clergy, professional soldier, and merchant class. Hume notes (vol. iii., chap. xxvi., p. 404) that the company of merchant adventurers in London had by their own authority debarred all other merchants of the kingdom from trading in the great marts of the Low Countries unless each trader previously paid to them the sum of near 70*l.*; a sum which at that date must have been almost prohibitive. At this time the trade to the Low Countries was the principal, if not the only, outlet for English exports. We can readily believe that this valuable monopoly was not maintained without due advantage being taken of it by the *protégés* and dependents of the ruling class.

There were, moreover, causes which operated to make the smaller tenants give up their holdings. When the famine was at its worst, rents, it is stated, fell, and land went out of cultivation. It was almost impossible to get land tilled on any terms. Yet, notwithstanding the extraordinary dislocation of trade, the price of provisions did not rise. Of course there were so many less mouths to feed, and the demand being less the price was less; but this consideration does not balance the enhancement of price which might have been expected to follow so terrible a catastrophe. By way of explanation, one might conjecture that in virtue of the Statute of Labourers there was some return to servile labour; it must also be remembered that landlords were capitalists, and where they could not force they hired labour. In this way labour was concentrated on certain portions of the land. The seasons besides were good and the harvest plentiful for the years following the great pestilence; small tenants also found they could make a larger income as labourers, and allowed their land to go out of cultivation and return to the waste. By means of this concentration of labour the supply of food was kept adequate to the population, and prices did not rise.

But the expedient of handing over his land to the capitalist farmer was not the only resource of the landlord. The English wool trade had always been a flourishing one, and English wool found a ready market in the Low Countries. Somewhat later a great impetus was given to the cultivation of wool by the rise of prices which took place about the middle of the sixteenth century. In 1349 and for nine years following the average price of wool was 7*s.* 1*d.* per tod of 28 lbs. In 1400–1430 the average price was 8*s.* 1½*d.* From 1431–1541 the average fell to 5*s.* 4½*d.*, and from 1541–1580 the average price was as high as 17*s.* 4*d.* There is evidence, moreover, that, notwithstanding this fluctuation in price, the wool trade was a profitable industry. The sheep farm requires very little hired labour, and if prices were remunerative the landlords were irresistibly drawn to turn their domain into pasture land. If we were to take the opinion of writers of the beginning of the sixteenth century we should be compelled to attribute the decay of prosperity entirely to the conversion of arable into pasture land. Undoubtedly this was one of the incidents which marked the reawakening of the landless labourer to the precariousness of his position, but the causes lay somewhat deeper. The element of change is one which must be reckoned with in the industry and commerce of any country. Our business is rather to investigate the causes which make an industrial country unfit to encounter a diversion of its industries into new and more profitable channels. It is not reasonable to attribute the suffering which generally accompanies these changes to the alteration in trade which is natural and inevitable, but we should rather refer it to some defect in the social condition of a people who cannot overcome a difficulty of almost everyday occurrence. The increased demand for English wool arose from certain natural, legitimate, and inevitable causes. Such difficulties as these must be encountered in all human progress. It is no explanation to say that the alleged decay of prosperity in the sixteenth century arose from the conversion of arable into pasture land. The question to be answered is: What was the condition of a people which allowed itself to be involved in misery and suffering by the diversion of its industries into more profitable channels? Before we attempt to answer this question, it may be desirable to make a short summary of the state of the country at the end of the fifteenth century. We have seen that, until the land had fully recovered from the mortality of the Death, and population had again reached its normal limit, there was naturally enough a very general state of content. The demand for labour was greater than the supply, and wages ruled high. Land was still widely held among small tenants, and all classes were well off. But amid this prosperity there were elements of decay. High wages had tempted men to leave their land and become labourers. Landlords were turning arable land into pasture, and were finding it profitable. There was thus less employment for labourers, and population was increasing and regaining its former numbers. It was inevitable that before long a pinch should come. The labourer was soon to find the labour market fully stocked, and the certainty of employment less. On the other hand, the soil, on which he once had a fixed though semi-servile tenure, had passed to other hands and to other purposes, and he could not again reinstate himself on the land. The landless labourer plying for hire had already become a feature in the social economy of rural England. His lot remained tolerable, so long as wages were high and employment plentiful, owing to the dearth of labour, but the vaunted prosperity of the time seems to have been doomed to vanish as soon as population recovered its former limit. If we pass from these details of the social condition of the country and survey for a moment the political events which distinguish the fifteenth century, we shall find much to corroborate the view which we have taken. The era under consideration commences with the accession of the house of Lancaster, and when it ends the Tudors were firmly seated on the throne. The period is filled up with a long series of civil and foreign wars. By the time of the seventh Henry the power of the feudal nobility had exhausted itself in war, and the enfranchisement of the villein was complete. Hume in his 23rd chapter describes the commutation of rents paid in service and in kind into the definite form of a fixed money lease, and proceeds :—

> After this manner villenage went gradually into disuse throughout the more civilised parts of Europe. The interest of the master as well as the slave concurred in this alteration. The latest laws which we find in England for enforcing or regulating this species of servitude were enacted in the reign of Henry VII.

As early as 1415, the military feudal system may be said to have broken down. At that date was held the first commission of array. The feudal obligations of the barons had been commuted, and no longer sufficed to supply the king with soldiers. Henry V. had to resort to a species of conscription in order to carry on his French wars. The rapacious and rigorous government of Henry VII. crushed still farther the power of the nobility, and consolidated the royal authority. There scarcely passed any session during this reign, says Hume, without some statute against inordinate retinues of retainers. There is a story of his remarking on the retinue of the Earl of Oxford, who entertained him at his castle of Heningham, 'By my faith, my lord, I thank you for your good cheer, but I cannot allow my laws to be broken in my sight. My attorney must speak with you.' Oxford is said to have paid 15,000 marks for this offence. The fall of the feudal nobility gave an opening for the rise of the lower classes of society. At the same time the baronage had been the principal check on the power of the Crown. On the ruin of the baronage rose the arbitrary power of the Crown. But in the meantime the peasantry profited by the change. The fifteenth century, says Mr. Freeman,[1] speaking from a constitutional point of view, was in some respects a time when things went back. Owing to this decay of the baronage, Parliaments were less independent than those of earlier times. A Parliament of Henry VI. passed the most reactionary measure that a parliament ever did pass that by which the qualification for a county elector was narrowed to those freeholders whose estates were of the yearly value of 40*s*. Forty shillings of that period is equivalent in modern value to 40*l*. The preamble to this statute rehearses that the county elections had been made by very great outrageous and excessive number of people dwelling

[1] *Growth of English Constitution*, p. 101.

within the same counties, of which most part was people of small substance.

In the following chapters, we must endeavour to follow the fortunes of this people of small substance, who had crept into property and freedom, and also those of the landless labourer who had gained freedom but not property during the period we have just surveyed.

CHAPTER V

THE INCREASE OF SHEEP-FARMING, AND THE GROWTH OF A PROLETARIATE

WE have already in the last chapter dwelt on the conversion of arable land into pasture, and on the enclosures of the waste for the purpose of sheep farming. We have assigned this phenomenon to what we believe to have been its real cause. It was a natural and inevitable step, resulting from the high price of labour and the profitable character of the industry of sheep-farming. In the social changes which this involved, the country was brought face to face with a difficulty which must sooner or later have made itself felt. Undoubtedly, labourers dependent solely on the sale of their labour suffered from the decrease of arable farming. So, at another time, operatives have been thrown out of work by changes in trade, and by the introduction of machinery. The process is a familiar one, even at the present day.

A contemplation of such incidents has provoked the modern socialist to say that the productive machinery of the country should be in the hands of

Government, and that industrial enterprise should be manipulated in the interest of the classes who have nothing but their labour to sell. The economist, on the other hand, points out that Government organisation of labour will not prevent changes in the currents and direction of trade, and insists that the right way for a people to meet these inevitable fluctuations is by giving increased facility for individual ownership, and that this can only be done by removing not by increasing the restrictions on the mobility of property. If the productive machinery of the country were vested in Government, society would be even more impotent than it is at present. It would be impossible for the State to adopt a new and improved system of manufacture or agriculture, because of the vested rights of those who were interested in old and antiquated methods of production. Change can best be encountered by that society in which property is most widely distributed. All men are there interested in the present state of things, but they will be also anxious to avail themselves of new markets, to turn their property to new uses, to adopt new machinery, and so decrease the demand on human toil. These are the conditions which make progress productive of health and happiness to all. It is the absence of these conditions that has made modern civilisation a by-word to the moralist, and a prey to the agitator.

At the period of which we are now speaking society had been brought face to face with one of the results of the impotence of the feudal system, that first attempt to administer property on a socialistic basis.

As we have seen, complete private ownership in land had been carefully made impossible. Yet owing to the natural self-assertion of the individual, labourers were creeping into freedom and property by means of copyhold tenure. The great labour famine, which followed the Black Death, threw all things into confusion, and gave effect to the divorce of population from property.

The creeping into freedom by means of property became less easy and less inviting than the manumission to be gained by hired labourers, through reliance on wagedom. The risks attached to property compared unfavourably with the certainty of continuous and well-paid work on the property of others. These circumstances established, as we have seen, the agricultural labouring class, and on the first important change of our national markets calamity was bound to overtake the unpropertied part of our population.

The moralists and popular politicians of a day when social phenomena had been but little studied, were entirely deceived by what they saw. They almost unanimously attribute the sufferings of the poorer classes at this date to the growth of sheep farming. It may be worth while to set out at some length the contemporary opinion of the subject. It has a strange resemblance to language which we hear at the present day, and it illustrates the fact that industrial crises are by no means of only modern occurrence, and further that though the occasion may be a change of trade, yet the causes lie much deeper, and remain a permanent menace to the prosperity of perhaps all known forms of industrial society.

A striking view of the situation is presented by Bacon, in his 'Life of Henry VII.' The king directed a statute of 'singular policy' to remedy some of the evils complained of.

> For enclosures at that time began to be more frequent, and arable land which could not be manured without people and families was turned into pasture, which was easily rid by a few herdsmen; and tenancies for years, lives, and at will, whereupon much of the yeomanry lived, were turned into demesnes. This bred a decay of people, and by consequence a decay of towns, churches, tithes, and the like. The king likewise knew full well, and in no wise forgot, that there ensued withal upon this decay a diminution of subsidies and taxes. *For the more gentlemen ever the lower books of subsidies.* For the remedying of this inconvenience the king's wisdom was admirable and the parliament's at that time.

The ordinance was that all houses of husbandry should be maintained and kept up for ever, together with a competent proportion of land, to be used and occupied with them. The penalty attached to neglect was forfeiture to the king. The object of the king, says Lord Verulam, was to prevent the disappearance of a middle class of people, who furnished in his opinion the best foot soldiers. For he argues :—

If a state run most to noblemen and gentlemen, and that the husbandmen and ploughmen be but as their work folks and labourers, or else mere cottagers who are but housed beggars, you may have a good cavalry, but never good stable bands of foot, and this is to be seen in France and Italy and some other parts abroad, where in effect all is noblesse or peasantry.

The passage quoted proves that the observant Henry VII., as early as the fourth year of his reign, saw the change which was coming about in the social condition of his people. The king had a shrewd eye to subsidies and good bands of foot. Cottagers and labourers are 'but housed beggars,' and the middle class of people the best payers of subsidy. Viewing the matter in the light of subsequent history, we see even more clearly than Henry and his great historian the importance of the crisis. A divorce of numbers from property was taking place. Our labouring classes were thrown back into a condition in which motives arising out of the possession of property had no play. A class of agricultural labourers depending solely on their labour was created. These supplied the towns, now growing into importance, with artisans, and when the industrial revolution of the eighteenth century dawned, a class of operatives was ready, accustomed to a bare maintenance, bereft for generations of all the prudent instincts of property, and willing to increase and multiply with a recklessness characteristic of a low state of civilisation. The progeny thus brought into the world were not subject to decimation by famine and pestilence, the natural scourges of a low condition of civilisation: the propertied classes stepped in, and by means of the employment given by an expanding trade, and where that failed by means of a compulsory poor law, maintained and fostered the growth of an unpropertied army of labourers.

The 'singular policy' of the astute monarch was, it need hardly be said, quite inoperative; and the complaint grew louder under the reign of his son. Sir Thomas More, writing in 1515–1516 in his 'Utopia,' speaks of the numbers of discharged soldiers and serving-men, who wander about the country. Thieving was so common that twenty men were hanged on one gallows. More reprobates this state of things, saying that men only thieve when they can do no better. He also 'checks landlords for rent-raising.' Another cause of stealing he goes on to say is:—

That your sheep, which were wont to be so meek and tame and so small eaters, now, as I hear say, be become so great devourers and so wild, that they eat up and swallow down the very men themselves. They consume, destroy, and devour whole fields, houses and cities. For look in what part of the realm doth grow the finest and therefore dearest wool, there noblemen and gentlemen, yea, and certain abbots, holy men no doubt, not contenting themselves with the yearly revenues and profits that were wont to grow to their forefathers and predecessors of their lands, nor being content that they live in rest and pleasure, nothing profiting, nay, much noying the public weal, leave no ground for tillage, they enclose all into pastures, they throw down houses, they pluck down towns, and leave nothing standing, but only the church to be made a sheep-house. . . . Therefore that one covetous and insatiable cormorant and very plague of his native country may compass about and enclose many thousand acres of ground together within one pale or hedge, the husbandmen be thrust out of their own, or else either by coveyn and fraud or by violent oppression they be put besides it, or by wrongs and injuries they be so weried that they be compelled to sell all; by one means therefore or another, either by hook or crook, they must needs depart away, poor, selye, wretched soules, men, women, husbands, wives, fatherless children, widows, woeful mothers with their young babes and their whole household, small in substance and much in number, as husbandry requireth many hands. All their household stuff which is very little worth, though it might well abide the sale; yet being suddenly thrust out, they be constrained to sell it for a thing of nought. And when they have wandered abroad till that be spent, what else can they do but steal, then justly pardy be hanged, or else go about a-begging, and yet then also they be cast in prison as vagabonds, because they go about and work not, whom no man will set to work, though they never so willingly profer themselves thereto. For one shepherd or herdsman is enough to eat up with cattle that ground to the occupying whereof about husbandry many hands were requisite. And this is also the cause why victuals be now in many places dearer. Yea, beside this the price of wool is so risen that poor folks who were wont to work it and make cloth thereof, be now able to buy none at all, and by this means very many be forced to forsake work and to give themselves to idleness. . . . And though the number of sheep increase never so fast, yet the price falleth not one mite, because there be so few sellers. For they be almost all comen to a few rich men's hands whom no need forceth to sell before they lust, and they lust not before they may sell as dear as they lust.

Such is the bitter cry uttered by one of the most eminent men of letters of the time. Nor is the picture drawn somewhat later, by the popular theologians of the day, much brighter.

Latimer, preaching some thirty years later (i.e. on March 8, 1549) before the new king, Edward VI., bitterly inveighs against the sins of the time. He spares not the king himself, nor the lawyer, nor the physician, nor the merchant, all of whom are inclined to seek 'too much' and to be covetous, and he thus addresses the landlords, whom he evidently thinks the worst offenders :—

You landlords, you rent-raisers, I may say you step-lords, you unnatural lords, you have for your possessions yearly too much. For that before went for 20*l.* or 40*l.* by year (which is an honest portion to be had *gratis* in one lordship of another man's sweat and labour), now is let for 50*l.* or 100*l.* by year. Of this cometh this monstrous and portentous dearth. . . . I tell you, my lords and masters, this is not for the King's honour. Furder more, if the King's honour (as some men say) standeth in the great multitude of people, then these grasiers, enclosers, and rent-rearers are hinderers of the King's honour. For where as have been a great many of householders and inhabitants, there is now but a shepherd and his dog, so they hinder the King's honour most of all. My lords and masters, I say also that all such proceedings, which are against the King's honour, ... do plainly intend to make the yeomanry slavery and the clergy 'shavery.' For such works are all singular private wealth and commodity. We of the clergy had too much, but that is taken away and now we have too little. But for mine own part I have no cause to complain, for I thank God and the King I have sufficient, and God is my judge I came not to crave of any man anything, but I know them that have too little. There lyeth a great matter by these impropriations; great reformation is to be had in them. I know . . . . the great gain goeth another way. My father was a yeoman and had no lands of his own; only he had a farm of iii. or iiii. pound by year at the uttermost, and hereupon he tilled so much as kept half a dozen men. He had walk for 300 sheep and my mother milked xxx. kine. He was able and did find the King a harness, with himself and his horse, while he came to the place that he should receive the King's wages. I can remember that I buckled his harness when he went into Black Heath Field. He kept me to school or else I had not been able to preach to the King's majesty now. He married my sisters with 5*l.* or 20 nobles a piece. . . . He kept hospitality for his poor neighbours and some alms he gave to the poor, and all this he did of the said farm. While he that now hath it payeth 16*l.* by the year or more, and is not able to do any thing for his prince, for himself, nor for his children, or give a cup of drink to the poor. Thus all the enhancing and rearing goeth to your private commodity and wealth. . . . But let the preacher preach till his tongue is worn to the stumps, nothing is amended. . . . In this realm there are a great many of folks ; amongst many I know but one of tender zeal, at the motion of his poor tenants hath let down his lands to the old rents for their relief. For Goddes love, let him not be a Phœnix. Let him not be alone, let him not be as a hermit closed in a wall, some good man follow him and do as he giveth example. Surveyors there be that greedily gorge up their covetousness, guttes hand makers I mean (honest men I touch not), but all such as survey they make up their mouths, but the commons be utterly undone by them. Whose bitter cry ascending to the God of Sabaoth, the greedy pit of hell burning fire (without great repentance) do tarry and look for them. A redress God grant. For surely there are but two things that do comfort me, I would despair of redress. One is that the King's majesty when he cometh to age, will be a redress to these things so out of frame. Giving example by letting down his own lands first and then enjoin his subjects to follow him. The second hope I have is that the general accompting day is at hand, the dreadful day of judgement I mean, which shall make an end of all these calamities and miseries.

Latimer in the above picture alludes to one important event on which it is necessary to say a few words. The dissolution of the monasteries proved without doubt a very serious dislocation to the rural economy of the country. In the first place, the religious houses were considerable employers of labour, and large purchasers of articles of commerce. A cessation of their custom must have been a serious blow to local industry. Further, they maintained a large retinue of serving men. It was one of the stock complaints of religious reformers that the monasteries were full of lazy worthless followers. With the suppression of the monasteries, all these men, whatever their character may have been, were thrown on the labour market. The charities of the monks had up to this date done all that was considered necessary for the relief of the poor. It is very possible that the action of the monks in this respect was not very discriminating, and that they only fostered the disease and increased the number of mendicants.

Old Fuller in his quaint way says of the Abbeys:—

Their hospitality was beyond compare. . . . Yet some will object that this their hospitality was but charity mistaken, promiscuously entertaining some who did not need, and more who did not deserve it. Yea, these abbeys did but maintain the poor which they made. For, some vagrants, accounting the abbey-alms their own inheritance, served an apprenticeship, and afterwards wrought journey work to no other trade than begging; all whose children were, by their father's copy, made free of the same company. Yea we may observe, that generally such places wherein the great abbeys were seated (some few excepted, where clothing began when their convent did end) swarm most with poor people at this day;[1] as if beggary were entailed on them, and that laziness not as yet got out of their flesh, which so long since was bred in their bones.

All this is confessed; yet by their hospitality many an honest and hungry soul had his bowels refreshed which otherwise would have been starved; and better it is two drones should be fed than one bee famished.

In any case this source of supply now ceased and prepared the way for the compulsory poor rate of Elizabeth. The confiscated revenues went, as Latimer says, not to the Church, but to the 'private wealth and commodity' of Henry and his favourites.

A further quotation from the racy and vigorous language of Latimer will bring us to the consideration of a grave crime of the legislature of the day.

In the same sermon, from which we have already made so long an extract, there occurs the following sentence:—

We have now a pretty little shilling, indeed a very pretty one. I have but one, I think, in my purse, and the last day I had put it away almost for an old groat, and so I trust some will take them. The fineness of the

[1] Fuller's *Church History*, published 1656, nearly 120 years after the suppression of the monasteries.

silver I cannot see, but therein is printed a fine sentence that is 'Timor Domini fons vitae vel sapientiae.' I would God this sentence were always printed in the heart of the King (in choosing his wife and in all his officers).

Preaching a fortnight later his third sermon before the King, Latimer tells his hearers that on account of this passage a gentleman had come up and charged him with sedition. 'I chanced in my last sermon to speak a merry word of the new shilling, to refresh my auditory . . . and I was herein noted to speak seditiously.' The preacher is content to shroud his invective under the guise of a 'merry word.' He is treading on very dangerous ground, but he dares to speak out and continues boldly to comfort himself that he is not alone. For was not the same accusation brought against Christ himself?

But (he goes on) I have gotten me one fellow more, a companion of sedition, and wot ye who is my fellow? Esai the prophet. I speak but of a little pretty shilling. But he speaketh of Jerusalem after another sort, and was so bold as to meddle with their coin. 'Thou proud, thou covetous, thou haughty city of Jerusalem. *Argentum tuum versum est in scoriam.* Thy silver is turned into what? Into testyons? *Scoriam*, into dross. Ah seditious wretch, what had he to do with the mint? Why should not he have left that matter to some master of policy to reprove? Thy silver is dross, it is not fine, it is counterfeit. Thy silver is turned, thou haddest good silver. What pertaineth that to Esai? Marry! he espied a piece of divinity in that policy; he threatened them

God's vengeance for it. He went to the rote of the matter, which was covetousness, which it became him to reprove, or else that it tended to the hurt of the poor people, for the naughtiness of the silver was the occasion of dearth of all things in the realm. . . . Was not this a seditious harlot to tell them this to their beards, to their face?

The preacher then, in order perhaps not to make his attack too personal to the King, inveighs against 'a certain cunning come up in mixing of wares.'

The clothiers (he says) rack their cloth from 18 to 27 yards, and when they have brought him to that perfection they have a pretty feat to thick him again. He calls me a powder for it and plays the pothecary; they call it floke powder, they do so incorporate it to the cloth.

The whole passage, which is worth consulting as an instance of pulpit eloquence and invective, concludes with another merry word against the 'same stout scornful gentleman' who laid sedition to his charge. Some explanation is necessary to make intelligible to the reader this 'merry word' of Latimer concerning the pretty little shilling.

In 1543, Henry VIII. had begun to debase the coinage. The debasement lasted only seventeen years, for in 1560 the standard was restored by Elizabeth, yet in Mr. Rogers' opinion ('Six Centuries of Work and Wages') the incident dominates the history of wages and labour. In 1549, the year of the sermon quoted, the shilling contained only $5\frac{1}{2}$*d.* worth of silver. In 1551 only $2\frac{3}{4}$*d.* Prices had, before this date, begun slowly and gradually to advance. One reason for this is to be found in the fact that silver was becoming cheaper, owing to the discoveries of the metal in Mexico, but the metals of the New World did not circulate freely till much later. The rise in prices may more naturally be referred to the ordinary growth of population, and to the fact that larger markets were being opened to English produce.

After the debasement of the coinage one or two abundant harvests prevented the price of wheat from rising, but very soon the mischief done began to appear. The price of meat and dairy produce rose to three times its former price. Corn became two and a half times as dear, but on the other hand the wages of labour rose but little. According to Mr. Rogers' calculation, a labourer's wages rose from 6*d.* to 9*d.* a day; but he had to pay 3*s.* for meat, 2*s.* 5*d.* for bread, and 2*s.* 6*d.* for butter and cheese, where before he only paid 1*s.* Thus, says Mr. Rogers, Henry gave effect to the Statute of Labourers. Direct legislation had hitherto failed to bring down the rate of wages, but the fraud now perpetrated, effectually and permanently reduced the labourer's wages. Previous to this debasement of the coinage, legal enactments for the purpose of controlling the rate of wages were inoperative, but, henceforward, the actual payments made appear to correspond with the rates fixed by the magistrates in quarter sessions, and, measured by their power of purchase, wages fell enormously.

The reason why wages do not at once rise on a debasement of the medium of exchange is not far to seek. If wages had been at their very lowest level, that is, just sufficient to give a bare maintenance to the labourer, a rise in the price of food would have necessitated a rise in wages, for otherwise labourers could not have existed. But the period of which we are now speaking was a time of tolerable prosperity, and the labourer's standard of life was such as to secure him a certain amount of rude comfort. Wages, therefore, were, as indeed they always are, something above the amount necessary to give a bare maintenance.

With a depreciation of the medium of exchange, the price of food and commodities rises, but the wages of labour are not so sensitive. They are regulated rather by custom than by the higgling of the market. Such custom has much the same effect as a contract. Much commiseration would be felt for a man who had contracted to deliver certain commodities to a purchaser, if during his contract the value of the coinage, in which he was to receive payment, had been debased about 75 per cent. But this is what really happened to the labourers of the time of Henry VIII.

The fraud was not understood at the time by those who suffered most by it, and their sufferings were attributed to other causes.

By the time that the effect of debasement had passed away there was, by reason of the extension of sheep-farming, less demand for labour. The dearth of employment was so serious that before the end of the century the poor law of Elizabeth was found necessary, and the labourer was beginning to exchange the servitude of the feudal system for the slavery and dependence of pauperism.

As a practical illustration of the alteration which these various causes had brought about in the condition of the English labourers, the following figures are cited from Mr. Rogers' work so often quoted. In 1495, during the prosperous times, wheat was 4*s.* 0¾*d.* per quarter, malt 2*s.* 4½*d.*, oats 1*s.* 7½*d.*, and oatmeal 5*s.* 4*d.* a quarter. An artisan earned 3*s.* a week, and a labourer 2*s.* In a year like this an artisan could provide his family with 3 quarters of wheat, 3 of malt, 2 of oatmeal, by working 10 weeks, a labourer could do the same by working 15 weeks.

In 1533, 4*s.* a week was paid to artisans, and 2*s.* to labourers. Wheat was 7*s.* 8*d.*, malt 5*s.* 5¼*d.*, oatmeal 8*s.*, oats 2*s.* 9½*d.* The labourer would have to work 30 weeks and the artisan 15 weeks to obtain the same provision.

In 1564, labourers' wages (as fixed by the magistrates of Rutland and confirmed as being the amounts actually paid to labourers at Oxford and Cambridge in this year) were about 3*s.* 6*d.* per week. Wheat was 19*s.* 9¾*d.*, oats 7*s.*, malt 10*s.* 8*d.*, and the labourer would take about forty weeks to earn his necessary provision. In 1593, wheat was at 18*s.* 4½*d.* The magistrates of the East Riding of Yorkshire fix a rate of wages at which the work of a whole year would not give a labourer the chance of earning the provision named. In 1597, wheat rose to 56*s.* 10½*d.* per quarter, that is to say, to three times the price of 1593; it is difficult to see how the labourer was able to exist at all during the year. In 1610, wheat was at 40*s.* 4*d.* per quarter, and the artisan to obtain the limit of maintenance named must work 43 weeks for it, but the labourer could not secure a maintenance even if he worked continuously the whole year through.

Mr. John Hales, one of the commissioners to redress enclosures, appointed on January 2, 1548, gives the following testimony :—

To defeat these statutes, as we be informed, some have not pulled down their houses, but maintain them, howbeit no person dwelleth therein, or if there be, it is but a shepherd or a milkmaid, and convert the land from tillage to pasture, and some, about one hundred acres of ground or more or less, make a furrow and sow that and the rest they till not, but pasture their sheep. And some take the lands from their houses and occupy them in husbandry, but let the houses out to beggars and poor old people. Some to colour the multitude of their sheep father them on their children, kinsfolk, and servants. All which be only crafts and subtilties to defraud the laws, such as no good man will use but rather abhor.[1]

The first portion of this complaint refers of course to the evasion of the legislation of Henry VII., which we have already cited. The latter part is in allusion to an Act passed in 1533, which limited the number of sheep which each owner might possess.

We must quote one more contemporary authority, namely Thomas Lever, who in a sermon preached at St. Paul's on Feb. 2, 1550, complains of rich merchants buying farms out of the hands 'of worshipful gentlemen, honest yeomen and poor labouring husbands, yea, they now buy also parsonages and benefices.' He further laments that the confiscated property of the monasteries is now turned to maintain 'worldly wicked covetous ambition.' Again, it is worthy of remark that gentlemen take higher rents, but it is even more wonderful to see husbandmen *offering* fines and higher rents for covetousness to get other men's land. The same preacher also tells us that it was a common custom with covetous landlords to let their housing so decay that the farmer may be fain for a small reward or none at all to give up his lease, that they taking the ground into their own

[1] Arber, xii. 12, *Lever's Sermons*.

hand may turn all to pasture, 'so now old fathers, poor widows, and young children lie begging in the miry street.'

It would be easy to multiply quotations, showing the pessimist views of contemporary writers. But Mr. Cunningham, in his erudite work on the 'History of Industry and Commerce,' is probably nearer the truth when he attributes much of the prosperity of the fifteenth century to the increase of sheep-farming. For undoubtedly there arose from this cause a great increase of what Latimer calls 'private wealth and commodity.' Nor does it appear to be true that tillage suffered. Exportation of corn was permitted, and owing to the better system of cultivation the price of corn did not rise. The most intelligent view of the situation from a contemporary source is that presented to us by ('W. S.') W. Stafford in a 'Compendious and Brief Examination of Certaine Ordinary Complaints,' printed in 1581, and also in Vol. ix. of the 'Harleian Miscellany.' The paper is a series of conversations between a learned doctor, a knight, a husbandman, and several tradesmen.

The husbandman complains of his rent, and of his landlord turning all to pasture, the capper that he has to pay his journeymen *2d.* per day more, and that twenty cities have fallen into decay. The merchant also agrees that towns are decayed and everything dearer. 'Yet I never saw more plenty of corn, grass, and cattle of all sorts.' The knight or landlord then urges that the cause of the dearth cannot be the enclosures, 'for corn is good, cheap, and hath been so these many years;' he confesses, however, that things are dearer, and that it is very hard on him who has only his lands to live on. 'You others have your trades and can raise your prices!' 'Yes,' says the husbandman, 'but you have raised your rents,' in which sentiment they all agree; the merchant adds, 'Yes, it was never merry with poor craftsmen since gentlemen became grasiers.' To this the knight replies, 'Yes, I do enhance my rent when I can, but the great part of my land is held by lease or copy granted out of my time, and as we have to pay more for everything so we have to keep part of our own lands or purchase farms for sheep-feeding. For we must needs increase our income.' The merchant then explains that 'This dearth has been ever since that basenesse of our English coin which happened in the later years of Henry VIII.' The doctor sums up and acknowledges that prices have risen all round, but as most of them participate in the rise of price he does not see how they can suffer. The persons who suffer are those whose living is rated at a certainty, e.g. common labourers at 8*d.* a day, journeymen of all occupations, and gentlemen whose lands are let on leases. They all agree that the doctor is a wise man, and invite him to discourse further on the matter. The conclusion of it all is that trade is setting towards sheep-farming to raise wool for the foreign market. The only remedy is to put a heavy tax on the export of wool. The situation is summed up in a sentence which might have come from the 'Wealth of Nations':—'Every man will seek where most advantage is, and they see there is more advantage in grazing and breeding than in husbandry and tillage by a great deal; and so long as it is so the pasture shall ever encroach upon tillage for all the laws that can be made to the contrary.' We have it also from Holinshed, writing generally of the reigns of Elizabeth and her father, that though corn was dear it was very plentiful.[1]

We are not, however, disposed to deny the disorders which had crept into society; but it is idle and misleading to talk of 'covetousness.' We have endeavoured to assign the results under consideration to their proper cause, namely, to the restrictions which the feudal system had placed on the mobility of property. Let us for a moment consider how the question of rent appears to stand.

1. Leases for terms of years and copyholds are still in force, and the landlord's legal right to 'enhance,' when occasion offers, does not appear to be disputed.

2. On the other hand, rather vague considera-

[1] Cf. Holinshed, i. 283.

tions of equity are set up by the preachers. Landlords are enjoined to let their land as did Latimer's phœnix landlord, at a lower price than the market warranted. Tenants too are blamed for offering to give more for a farm than a sitting tenant.

3. There is the common sense idea that agriculture is a matter of business, and that landlords, like other people, will seek where their advantage is, and sell or lend their property at the best market rate, and that contracts of tenancy must be observed.

English agriculture has suffered, and continues to suffer, from this confusion of ideas, and impotence has in consequence fallen on this most important industry. Undoubtedly the manorial system, as we have shown, in a sense arose out of an usurpation, but it is so old a story that a fresh act of injustice would do more harm than good. The problem, then, was how land was to be turned to its most profitable use without undue injury to the equitable rights of labourers whose interest lay in the old unprofitable form of culture. At that time the interest of the labourer was neglected, with the result we have seen. To-day a different question arises, which has, however, its origin in the same confusion of ideas. Legislation, to some extent, and public opinion have conferred on the tenant as well as on the landlord an equitable property in the land, and the result is that there is full security for investment to neither landlord nor tenant; as a consequence the land is starved, and farmers, in close propinquity to the largest market in the world, are crying out for protection.

CHAPTER VI

TOWN LIFE AND THE TRADE GILDS

WE have hitherto confined ourselves to a consideration of rural life. Undoubtedly this was for long the most important aspect of English society, but it is necessary before going further to say something of the condition of the mediæval town.

A few of the towns were survivals from Roman times, but, as is well known, the Saxon invasion broke entirely the continuity of town life—many towns lay for centuries in ruins. Some have been repaired, but others, such as Silchester (Calleva) and Pevensey (Anderida), lie in ruins to this day.

Other towns grew up round the monasteries. Oxford owed its first origin to the religious houses of St. Frideswide and Oseney, and to its university. Abingdon, Reading, St. Albans, Coventry, Durham and York owe their existence to the ecclesiastical associations for which they are famous. Bristol, Norwich, and Southampton were important by reason of their convenience for trade. Yarmouth, Grimsby, and Scarborough were early famous for their fishing. As has been already pointed out, in the early times the capitalist tradesman did not exist. Artisans possessed no stock beyond their tools; the raw material which they were to work up was supplied by the customer. Merchants and shopkeepers, except in the large towns, did not exist for the purpose of supplying the country with commodities. The rural population received its supplies from periodical fairs and from the travelling packman. The merchant was a person who traded abroad. The essential feature of the mediæval town society was the gild, and of this important and interesting institution we must attempt to give some account, in so far as it concerns the status of the labourer.

It is generally said that the gild is a development of the ancient 'Frith-borh' or peace-pledge, which was a well-known feature in the Saxon community. A family through its headman or lord was called on to give Frith-borh for its members. It was at once a protection and a guarantee of good conduct. Communities bound together by this peace-pledge existed long before the incorporation of townships. It is rather tempting to identify this embryo form of the town gild with the village community in the rural districts, and to assume that the same germ, which in the country developed into the manorial system, in places where circumstances made for town rather than for rural industry grew into the gild. The incorporation of these communities into townships was merely a legalisation of an institution which already existed. The origin of the name gild connects it with the payment of gelt or money as a part of membership. Mr. Toulmin Smith found in one bundle in the British Museum accounts of upwards of 500 of these mediæval gilds. These returns were drawn up in execution of an order made in the reign of Richard II., in Nov. 1388. The earlier records are in Old French, and the later ones are in English. From this source most of our knowledge is derived.

The gilds in their organised form may be described as associations for mutual help. They are divided into social gilds, merchant gilds, craft gilds. The social gilds were for the most part religious in their character, and are somewhat outside our purview. It is a remarkable circumstance pointing, one might argue, to the family origin of the institution, that scarcely five out of the five hundred gilds excluded women from membership The gild members, especially one might imagine in the social gilds, were very numerous. The Corpus Christi gild at York is said to have had as many as 14,850 members. The other gilds were more of the nature of trade protection societies. The gild merchant, having the care of the general trading interests of the community, not unnaturally stood at the head of the town gilds. Craftsmen were not excluded from this gild, but the tendency after a time was to confine membership to the richer tradesmen and masters of industry. Even in the time of Edward III. the richer gilds had begun to separate themselves from the poorer associations of craftsmen, as in the case of the Grocers Company of London, who received their name as being buyers *en gros*. Incorporation as a township was sometimes granted to a merchant gild. In London the gilds united for purposes of defence, and so formed the corporation. The same is said to have happened at Berwick. The origin of craft gilds is sometimes referred to the Roman *collegia opificum*, but the weight of probability seems rather to identify them with communities of bond craftsmen on episcopal or other large estates. These craftsmen were subject to a lord, who appointed an officer for the protection of the industry of his servants. It is probable that at first free handicraftsmen belonged to the full citizen or merchant gilds, but in course of time, as above stated, the merchant gilds came to consist of the successful masters of industry, and the mere handicraftsman was expelled. By the fourteenth century the merchant gilds were already capitalist societies. Membership was hereditary, and their principal object was to maintain their own monopoly. The accumulation of property enabled the gild brethren to live idly. There came therefore to be a strong rivalry between the higher and lower order of gilds. The craft gilds were excluded from the management of municipal affairs till the 49 Edward III., when they established their right to be the electors of the civic dignitaries. By the time of Henry VI. incorporation of townships was ceasing to be granted by confirmation of merchant gilds in their assumed supremacy, but was bestowed in favour of the community generally. Although there was this rivalry between the various gilds, they all united in attempting to secure a monopoly of trades and markets. The country population was prevented from flocking to the towns to seek employment except at such times and places as labour was required. They protected also their own members from the competition of strangers. Heavy fines and entrance fees were exacted, and proof of suitable birth was also required as a qualification for membership. Prohibitive terms of apprenticeship were maintained, and journeymen were obliged to travel to prevent too much competition or a reduction of the profits and wages of trade. In certain places, no doubt, when there was a considerable demand for labour, the rich employers relaxed their rules and received labourers from the country. The emancipation resulting from membership in a town gild has already been noted as one of the principal solvents of the servile condition of the rural labourer. The inquisition of Richard II., already mentioned, was without doubt undertaken because of the abuses to which the gild system had given rise. In the sixteenth century the gilds were entirely in the hands of the richer members, and were little more than capitalist trading companies limiting production to enhance their own profits. To escape from the tyranny of the gilds trade forsook the chartered towns and migrated to new districts, and complaints arose as to the decay of towns. The country people began to follow the industries which had hitherto been the staple of the town, and legislation was called in to protect the monopoly of manufacture and market claimed by the gilds of the town. There is scarcely a town in England which is excepted by the pessimists of the day from the list of the decayed towns of England. Henry VIII., when he had spent the money wrested from the Church, proceeded to confiscate the possessions of certain fraternities, brotherhoods, and gilds. These were, by the 37 Henry VIII. c. 4, vested in the Crown under the plea that they should be used to more godly and virtuous purposes. A further enactment, 1 Edward VI. c. 14, completed the confiscation. The London gilds were saved, and survived to a later day. Those of them which retained an industrial character were crushed by the advance of industrialism in the eighteenth century. Some of them, like the Frame Work Knitters, dispersed their endowments in an ineffectual attempt to oppose machinery and progress. This briefly is the history of the trade gilds. It is very clear that they had fallen away from the ideal purpose which historians impute to them, namely, the purpose of protecting labour. Originally this undoubtedly was their object; but by a principle of degeneration only too common in human associations they had resolved themselves into close corporations, from which the poorer workmen were excluded. This failure of mediæval associations of labour is in our view analogous to the failure of the communism of the village community and of feudalism in regulating the economy of rural life. In the first place, no corporation can fully understand, and, not fully understanding, cannot protect all the interests of all its members. The only safeguard is to be found in individual freedom and individual self-assertion. Not only are corporations unable to manage effectively the affairs of their own members, but they have absolutely no control over those who are not of their body. Population increases, and classes of men arise who are not admitted as members of a gild or corporation. The interest of the gild is actually inimical to these fresh competing groups of workmen.[1] The energy of western civilisation

[1] There is a modern analogy in the conflicting interests which arise in the course of a strike. In 1886 an arbitration composed the differences between employers and employed in the Tyne and Wear ship building trade, but the terms of peace made no provision for the case of the unskilled labourer, who perforce joined in the strike, but without the aid of trade union funds. Further, considerable distress occurred in allied trades, and charitable subscrip-

has swept away the barriers of trade gilds, but in India the caste system has taken hold of the national life of the country, and, it is needless to say, has altogether failed to solve the problem of an equitable distribution of the products of industry.

As already stated, the incorporation of a town was very often merely the record of the existence and legal validity of the principal gild or confederation of gilds, but in later times the charters were granted to the whole body of burgesses. From the king's point of view, it was desirable that trade should centre in one or two places, so that the work of his tax-gatherers should be easier. A valuable consideration had to be paid for the privilege of market and trade. Gilds claiming a monopoly without due authority were fined. The dues of the market were collected originally by the officer of the gild or by the king's sheriff. Later on the corporation paid a fixed sum, and so became an independent body. The officer of the gild appears to have been appointed by the bishop or lord, who granted incorporation to his servants. Mr. Cuningham points out that the term 'mystery' so often applied to the ordinances of a gild is an etymological error. The real word

tions were raised to meet it, but the unfortunate unskilled labourer above mentioned was excluded from participation. Obviously also a strike of coal miners causes a dislocation of trade and enforced idleness of workmen far beyond the circle controlled by the Miners Union. – See Price, *Industrial Peace* (Macmillan & Co.)

is 'mestier,' ministerium, service or servitude, and points to the semi-servile origin of the gild. It was, as already noted, esteemed by the Church a virtue to grant manumission to serfs, and the granting of a charter in return for a valuable consideration was at once a good stroke in trade as well as in theology. During the crusades barons who wished to raise money for their expedition not unfrequently resorted to this device. Rye and Winchelsea received charters for supplying ships for Richard I.'s expedition to the Holy Land, and Portsmouth and Norwich for paying a portion of his ransom.

The life of the poorer workmen in towns previous to the seventeenth century remains a very obscure question. Industry was then carried on in the household; spinning, weaving, bleaching, were the home occupations of the peasantry and artisans. Capital as yet had not been applied to industry. The produce of industry was therefore small and served only for the home market. The export trade was confined to the raw material, principally wool, and at times grain. What the modern world now understands by investment did not exist. The use of money for any purpose other than expenditure was termed usury, and discountenanced both by law and religion. The labourer's tools were his own, and so far he was his own capitalist. In some instances also he bought his own raw material; it is one of the complaints of the writers of the sixteenth century that wool had grown too dear for the poor weaver to buy. In other words, the small weaver could not even entertain the idea of applying capital to the advancement of industry.

The towns on the southern coast exported tin and other metals. The eastern counties sent corn to Norway, and the Cinque Ports were the channels of trade to Flanders. The prosperity of the town was the prosperity of a trading rather than of a manufacturing population. History is very silent as to the suffering of the poor of the mediæval town. In Mr. Brewer's preface to the 'Monumenta Franciscana,' some light is thrown on this obscure subject. The mission of St. Francis and his followers was to the poor of the towns. It is often asserted that, as the wages of artisans were higher than those of labourers, the general status of the town population was superior to that of the country labourer. It appears to be true that municipal institutions and a certain amount of self-government existed in the towns, long before history gives us any trustworthy account of the social condition and material prosperity of the people, and this preserved the population from being brutalised by the squalor, ignorance, and poverty of their surroundings; but there is much to warrant Mr. Brewer's view that the position of the inhabitant of the town was in those days inferior to that of the peasant. The streets were narrow and winding, and served as a protection to violent men. Among the houses were ditches and ponds full of garbage, and the houses themselves were wooden sheds rudely plastered. Here leprosy and the plague entered. The city ponds and rivulets gave fresh water to those who went to fetch it. The chaplain of the gild provided for religious worship, and the common purse of the gild furnished relief against misfortune. 'But for the ungilded population, which resided in the suburbs, there were no such advantages. Imagination can only conceive their condition. History is silent.'

Poverty is always an evil, but it seems to have a less repellent air in the country than in the town. A healthy animal life is possible in the country. A town is a product of civilisation, and the contrasts between wealth and destitution seem more artificial, more clearly the result of human incapacity, and the situation appears to us more lamentable.

On the other hand, the peasant is more apathetic, more contented to go on as his fathers before him. The life of a rural labourer is in many ways an archaic survival. The changing industrial conditions which have altered the face of the country, have had comparatively little effect on him. Provincial dialects have brought down to us forms of speech which were current centuries ago among both rich and poor. This archaic language, as well as these archaic habits and traits of character, remain intact among our rural poor. The classes which have been caught and whirled by the stir and energy of modern life have acquired new habits and new speech.

But while the poor in town and country have distinct characteristics, in their history as a class there are many points of analogy. The village community and its later development, the manorial system, arose out of the natural instinct which compels men to act in concert, one family against another family, one group against another group. The confederation, originally based on family ties and for purposes of self-preservation, became a confirmed system of slavery for those who lived within its influence. The gild has, in some instances, undoubtedly its origin in the association of the servile bondsmen of a great temporal or spiritual lord. The combination was made with the approval of the lord, and for the protection of his servants against the servants of other lords. But at a very early stage of their history the gilds, or corporations, fell away from their original purpose, and remained only as obstacles to the free progress of industry.

At the same time it is often argued that the manorial system, with its waste land and commons for the use of the poor on the one hand, and on the other the gilds and mediæval trade protection societies, played a useful and perhaps a beneficent part in advancing civilisation. They grew up to meet a difficulty, but when the difficulty was overcome they remained to block the way to further progress. Communism in landed property was perhaps necessary to prevent one family from encroaching on another, but in the long run it prevented any mobility in the ownership of land. In this way it has bequeathed to successive generations a legacy of obstruction from which, even at the present day, it is impossible to escape. The early institution of the gild had also its use; it protected industry from its foes in a way that the State was unable to do. But when times grew more peaceful and incorporation was no longer absolutely necessary, the restrictions of gilds and corporations appear to have driven trade to seek for a freer atmosphere. The gilds found it impossible to extend their ranks so as to include a growing population, over whose increase and conduct they had absolutely no control.

The failure of these various forms of socialism appears to strengthen our contention that society must rest on an individualistic basis. Association to produce a certain result is useful and salutary for the moment, but associations cannot adapt themselves to changing circumstances, and have no final and permanent control over individual action and springs of conduct. Social disorders are produced by the action of individuals, and must be cured by the same means. Undoubtedly unjus and inexpedient laws aggravate the evil and demoralise the individual. But laws have no power to control the rate at which population increases, nor the use which people make of the money or wealth which they earn. The motives which govern population and expenditure utterly elude the provisions of the law, they must rest on individual self-control. Yet these are the two questions which dominate the whole subject of a proper adjustment of population to wealth. The creed of socialism is that this adjustment can be brought about by the action of the State. We venture to say, however, that hitherto all experience seems to teach the futility of this view. The tendency towards deterioration in collectivist institutions has been proved in smaller and less important instances, but we refer with some confidence to the colossal failure of the feudal system, and of the incorporated mediæval trade societies as capital instances of the impossibility of adjusting wealth and population by any socialistic formula.

CHAPTER VII

SOCIAL LEGISLATION AND THE POOR LAW

CONCURRENTLY with the history of industrial progress we must also study the poor law legislation of the country. For this legislation has exerted a most important effect, not only on the economy of English life, but, what is far more important, on the character and habits of the English labourer.

Causes which we have attempted to describe regulated the distribution of property among the people of this country, and, as we have seen, individuals and even classes were divorced from a participation in property. These persons became dependent solely on the labour of their hands, and at the first important change in the course of our national trade a great want of employment, and consequent destitution, occurred. To meet this state of things, from time to time resort has been had to legislation. Legislation with regard to the poor in England has proceeded from many different motives, and some enquiry into its origin and necessity cannot fail to be instructive.

The connection of poor law relief with our parochial system dates from the very earliest times. We have already quoted the law of Athelstane, p. 46. Such an enactment was in its origin a measure of police. The humanitarian aspect of the poor law is of much later date. The object of early legislation was to enforce the principle that every man had a settlement in some manor or parish, and that each manor or parish should be held responsible for the conduct and good behaviour of its inhabitants. Further, this subordination of all men to manorial jurisdiction was a perquisite or right of the lord of the manor, and one which for long it was worth his while to maintain. Again, the town gilds somewhat jealously watched the migrating labourer from the country; at times his labour may have been welcome, but more often he was sent back to the place where 'he oweth to serve.' Undoubtedly, however, this ascription to the soil tended to confer certain equitable but undefined rights of maintenance on the labourer; but, as already remarked, early legislators were barely able to protect the rich in the possession of their property, and the interest of the destitute was never considered. In this way, however, the duty of providing for its poor became more and more explicitly recognised by the community, till at length it culminated in the institution of the modern poor law in the 43rd of Elizabeth. With the decay and gradual abolition of servitude, the rights as well as the duties of the lord of the manor disappeared; and when the old order of things changed the duty of caring for the poor was by a not unnatural division of labour thrown on the Church; which, following the precepts of Christian charity, had already undertaken the distribution of the alms of the benevolent. Regarded from an ecclesiastical point of view the manor is the parish, and from henceforth the parish, originally a less important division of the land than the manor, has determined the area of poor law jurisdiction even under the form of the modern union. It would be too long to follow in detail all the legislation which bears upon the social condition of the labourer; it will suffice to indicate its course in broad outline. During the reign of Richard II. the statute book bears evidence to the struggle for emancipation which was going on. The conflict was attended with some amount of lawlessness. Large numbers of men were being drawn into the towns, which had advanced in prosperity during the firm government of Edward III.; and for this cause, as well as on account of the decimation of numbers by the plague, there was a dearth of labourers in the country. The laws aimed at preventing these migrations of labour, and strove to bind each man to follow his own trade, in his own place, and even attempted to make the children follow the calling of the parents. Penalties were enacted against mayors and officers of towns for harbouring labourers whose labour was due to a master on the land. The conflict culminated in the rebellion of Wat Tyler, 1381. Two years after this rebellion the legislation against vagabonds recommences.

In 1388 was passed an Act which is generally regarded as the introduction of a poor law, namely, the 12 Richard II. It forbids the migration of labourers, male or female; if a servant is found wandering in a town or borough, he shall be taken and put in the stocks until he hath found surety to return to his service or to serve in the place from whence he came. Not only country labourers, but also servants, artificers, and apprentices, shall be compelled to serve in harvest, to cut, gather, and bring in the corn. A scale of wages is of course fixed, as demands are said to be excessive.

It is constituted an offence to take or give more wages than the Act allows.

The statute then orders that the able-bodied beggar shall be treated as one who has wandered from his service, but, and this is the first instance of what we may call the humanitarian aspect of the poor law, 'Beggars impotent to serve' must abide in the places where they were at the time of the proclamation of this statute, and if the people will not or cannot 'find them,' they must go elsewhere or to the towns where they were born and dwell there continually. It is worth noting that, although the impotent poor are distinguished as a separate class, and though they are exempted from the rigour of the law, no definite provision is made for them.

In 15 Rich. II. cap. 6, 1392, it was enacted that on the appropriation of the revenues of any parish church to a cathedral or other corporation, 'the diocesan shall ordain a convenient sum of money to be distributed yearly of the fruits and profits of the same to the poor parishioners in aid of their living and sustenance for ever.' Thus even at this date the care of the impotent poor was held to be the responsibility of the Church, and the Act was intended to protect the interest of the poor in the event of the parish being served by a non-resident priest from the chapter or monastery to which the revenues belonged. A resident priest might be expected to do his duty in such matters, though of course he was under no legal compulsion to do so.

The repression of wandering from servitude still continues to be the principal object in social legislation, and it turns much on the conflicting interest of town and country. In the 7 Henry IV. cap. 17, passed in 1406, the following passage occurs :—

Notwithstanding the good statutes afore made infants whose fathers and mothers have no land, nor rent, nor any other living, but only their service or mystery, are put to serve and bound apprentice to divers crafts within cities and boroughs sometimes at the age of twelve years, sometimes within the same age, and that for the pride of clothing and other evil customs that servants do use the same; so that there is great scarcity of labourers and other servants of husbandry, that the gentlemen and other people of the realm be greatly impoverished for the cause thereof, for remedy whereof it is ordained . . . that no man or woman of what estate soever, shall put their son or daughter of whatsoever age to serve as apprentice to no craft nor other labour within any city or borough except he have land or rent to the value of 20*s*. by the year at the least.

The object of all this is apparent; the socialism of the day wanted to make agricultural labour plentiful and cheap and to give permanence to the feudal ideal. This legislation made an outlaw of every independently-minded labourer who escaped from villenage in an unauthorised way, and naturally increased the number of vagrant and lawless men. The long French wars of Henry V. must have given honourable employment to many of these outlaws. We can readily believe that his recruiting commissioners of array (see p. 69) did not examine too closely the validity of a freeman's deed of manumission, and that the able-bodied evader of service found enlistment an honourable retreat from his predicament. The French wars carried off the majority of the rural gentry, and in 1421, from the preamble of 9 Henry V. cap. 5, it would appear that there was lack of 'valiant and sufficient persons' in many of the English counties 'to occupy and govern the same' owing to the ravages of pestilence and war. The King therefore is empowered to create fresh officers and sheriffs to carry on the business of the country.

We may imagine that this exhaustion of the country gave a respite to the hunting of the peasant who evaded his service, and from this time forward the battle seems rather to rage over the question of the regulation of wages and apprenticeship, and over attempts to degrade the labourers' standard of living by repressive sumptuary laws. To this latter point some importance should be attached. We shall have occasion, in another portion of this work, to consider the influence of the standard of living in determining the condition and wages of labour.

In 1427, in the 6 Henry VI. cap. 3, occurs a curious admission of the futility of all this repressive legislation and attempts to regulate the rate of wages. It is recited that the statutes punishing masters for giving more than the statutory wages are too hard, 'for as much as they shall be destitute of servants, if they should not pass the ordinance of the statute,' and pay more than the law permits. It is then made the duty of the justices to fix by proclamation at Easter and Michaelmas the wages of labour. By the same statute London, 'in virtue of its entire affection to our lord the King,' was exempted from the operation of the law which forbade the apprenticeship of children in towns. In 1444 a very elaborate Act was passed, regulating in great detail the wages of different labourers and artisans, and fixing penalties for evasion of the Act.

After the accession of the House of York in 1463, by the 3rd Edward IV. cap. 5, legislation descends to a regulation of clothing to be worn by different ranks. Nineteen years later complaint is made that this Act was not observed, and that great misery and poverty was in some way the consequence; they therefore proceed to pass another ordinance of clothing. These regulations applied to all ranks of society, and prescribed the dress of the bishop and the noble, as well as of the peasant and the artisan.

When we reach the time of the Tudor dynasty the tide was turning the other way. The landlords no longer wished to have labourers on their land. Sheep-farming had become profitable. Legislation against vagrancy still continues. The 11 Henry VII. cap. 2 is an Act against vagabonds and beggars The charges for imprisonment had become very heavy, and some variation in punishment seemed necessary. Impotent beggars are to reside in their own hundred, and not to beg out of the hundred.

In 1495 the apprenticeship laws were relaxed in favour of Norwich, and later in favour of all

Norfolk, at that date a principal seat of the woollen trade, for the great crafts of the city were decayed for want of labour, and surplus labour was becoming an embarrassment in the country.

In the same year Acts were passed for the further regulation of wages, and for fixing the hours of labour. From the middle of March to the end of September, the hours were from five in the morning to seven or eight at night, with half-an-hour for breakfast and an hour and a half for dinner and sleep. During the winter, that is from September to March, labourers were to be at their work 'at the springing of day and depart not till night,' and only one hour is allowed for dinner.

The situation is now entirely changed; the cry is no longer that of the landlords who are deprived of their labourers, but of the labourers who can get no one to hire them, and who have lost their customary tenure on the land. Even the increasing trade of the towns could not absorb all the labour thrown on the market by the natural increase of the population, and by the labour-saving institution of the sheep-farm. An Act of 1533 recites that—

> A marvellous multitude of the people of the realm be not able to provide meat, drink and clothes necessary for themselves, their wives and children, and be so discouraged with misery and poverty that they fall daily to theft, robbery, and other inconvenience, or pitifully die for hunger and cold.

The country was now suffering from over-population, or, at least, from a congestion of labourers in places where they were not required. It was no longer a coveted privilege for the owner of the soil to recall the errant labourer. The maintenance of the poor was becoming too large a question for the voluntary efforts of the Church. Even the towns were said to be falling into decay, as is recited in an Act passed in 1543. In 1511, an Act had been passed giving protection from foreign competition to some of the branches of the wool trade. No doubt also the poverty of the country people operated as a considerable check on the purchasing powers of the community at large. Probably, however, the statement of decay of towns is to be explained by the fact that the free course of trade sought other centres where industrial operations were not impeded by charters and gild monopolies. The old towns, too, were built for purposes of fortification, and were in many ways unsuited for trade.

In the 33 Henry VIII. cap. 15, we hear of the growing importance of Manchester.

The inhabitants are well set a work in making of cloths as well of linen as of woollen, whereby the inhabitants have obtained, gotten, and come into riches and wealthy living, and have kept and set many artificers and poor folk to work within the said town, and many poor folk had living and children and servants there, virtuously brought up in honest and true labour out of all idleness.

This and similar facts are the real explanation of the decay of some of the old chartered towns, and the loss of the old was more than made up by the growth and prosperity of the new. Still, a population, unabsorbed by the extension of trade, had been somehow called into existence, and remained a source of anxiety to the Government. The development of the law for the provision of the poor proceeds apace. The churchwardens are ordered to take discreet and convenient order to gather the alms of good Christian people. The parson, the vicar, and the curate are to exhort the people to charity. The churchwardens are to keep account of the incomings and outgoings of the fund. Sturdy vagabonds and 'rufflers' have new and varied punishments provided for them. Poor children are to be placed in situations where they may earn their living.

In the first year of Edward VI. branding with a hot iron, with a 'V' for vagrant, and 'S' for slave, was enacted as a fitting punishment. The children of vagrants are to be apprenticed, and the impotent poor recommended to the clergy. By an Act of the same reign, the parson's collectors are to demand of every man and woman in church what they of their charity will give for the relief of the poor and to enter the same in a book, and to distribute the same without fraud, covine, favour or affection, among the impotent poor. If a person is obstinate and froward, and refuse to give, the parson and churchwardens are gently to admonish him; and if he will not be persuaded, the bishop is to send for him, and take order according to his discretion. As a proof that vagabondage had attained great dimensions at this time, Sir G. Nicholls quotes a contemporary work, 'A Caveat or Warning for Common Cursetors vulgarly called Vagabonds,' published in 1566, wherein it appears that the vagabond class was a regular institution with a definite slang language of its own. London swarmed with rogues, vagabonds, and masterless men. All this is evidence of the growth of a very degraded population, but not necessarily of great depression of trade or want of employment, for a degraded population grows and multiplies with most alarming rapidity whenever a maintenance is by law or custom provided for it. But in thinking of this alleged evil of vagabondage, we must remember that the spirit and temper of the times was very different to the modern view. As an instance of this, we remind the reader that an Act of Henry VIII. addresses itself to a regulation of the begging of Oxford undergraduates, who are required to provide themselves with a licence before practising the art of begging.

Passing over many minor but yet important statutes, we come in 1601 to the famous 43 of

Elizabeth, which established a compulsory rate for the relief of the poor.

For long this legislation remained but slightly operative. In 1630, under the personal government of Charles I., a commission was appointed to see to the execution of the laws for the maintenance of the poor. For these laws, it was alleged, had not been carried into effect. The legal maintenance for the poor therefore had not yet become sufficiently general to create its own population.

In 1651 the legal rate of interest was reduced to six per cent., an evidence that wealth was accumulating. A further proof of the expansive nature of English industry is furnished by the fact that when after the Restoration the army was disbanded—some 50,000 or 60,000 men in a population not exceeding five millions and a half—these numbers melted away into the ranks of industrial society, without producing any crisis. The only special act of legislation was that for the disbanded soldier no apprenticeship was required to enable him to practise any trade he pleased. These facts might warrant us in supposing that a growing industrialism was equal to absorbing the increase of population, and that the neglect of the provisions of the 43 Elizabeth had saved the country as yet from a permanent pauper population.

In 1662 was enacted a Settlement Act, which prevented the migration of labour (14 Charles II.

cap. 12). This recites that owing to some defect in the law poor people are not restrained from going from one parish to another, and therefore do endeavour to settle themselves in those parishes where there is the best stock, the largest commons or wastes to build cottages, and the most woods for them to burn and destroy; it is enacted therefore that on the complaint of the churchwardens or overseers of any parish, persons settling in a parish and living in a tenement of less than 10*l.* yearly value, where they are likely to become chargeable, may be removed by order of the justices 'to such parish as where he or they were last legally settled.'

These mischievous restrictions have remained in operation to modern times. Their influence soon became felt. Roger North, writing about 1688, says:—

> Surely it is a great imprisonment, if not slavery, to a poor family to be under such restraint by law that they must always live in one place, whether they have friends, employment, or not, or however they might mend their condition by moving.

Again:—

> The poor are imprisoned in their towns and chained down to their wants, so that they are deprived of means to mend their condition, but if any chance to move for experiment they are then sent back and tossed from pillar to post in carts, till they return to their old settled misery again. No town willingly receives a poor man

though they want poor people to do the ordinary works of husbandry, because they say his family may become a charge to the parish.

The parish or manor no longer seeks to retain its own labouring poor, as an advantage to itself. Labour is rather a burden than a valuable commodity, and a parish is forced by the jealousy of its neighbours to keep the labourers who belong to it, whether they are required or not. An Act of 1685 recites 'that poor people at their first coming into a parish do commonly conceal themselves.' The enemy whom they sought to evade was not the superior to whom their labour was due, but the representative of the timid ratepayer in their new home, who feared that in course of time a new addition might be made to the rates. The remarks of Adam Smith on this iniquitous law of settlement have often been quoted (vol. i. 219, cap. 10) :—

To remove a man who has committed no misdemeanour from the parish where he chuses to reside is an evident violation of natural liberty and justice. The common people of England, however, so jealous of their liberty, but like the common people of most other countries never rightly understanding wherein it consists, have now for more than a century together suffered themselves to be exposed to this oppression without a remedy. . . . There is scarce a poor man in England of forty years of age, I will venture to say, who has not in some part of his life felt himself most cruelly oppressed by this ill-contrived law of settlements.

In 1697 a workhouse was established at Bristol. It was used as a test of destitution and was found to be successful to a moderate extent.

In 1782 an important Act, known as Gilbert's Act, was passed. It is entitled 'An Act for the better Relief and Employment of the Poor.' Section 29 provides that no person shall be sent to the poor-house except such as are become indigent by old age, sickness or infirmities. With respect to the rest of the poor, Section 32 provides that the guardians, if applied to, must

> agree for the labour of such poor person or persons at any work or employment suited to his or her strength and capacity, in any parish or place near the place of his or her residence, and to maintain or cause such person or persons to be maintained, lodged and provided for, until such employment shall be procured and during the time of such work, and to receive the money to be earned by such work or labour, and apply it in such maintenance as far as the same will go and to make up the deficiency if any.

Sir G. Nicholls points out that the poor-house was in no sense a workhouse, and with regard to Section 32 he sums up somewhat in the following terms:—

> It assumes that there can never be a lack of profitable employment, and the guardians must find it near the labourer's own cottage, where, if it existed, he might have found it for himself. The labourer is thus deprived of all motive to use diligence to bargain for his wages, for the guardian must make up the deficiency to him: he is

certain of employment and is not called on to exercise forethought.

Could a more certain way be devised for lowering character, destroying self-reliance, and discouraging improvement?

An Act of 1722 had limited in a very slight measure the powers of justices to order relief independently of the overseers, and also empowered the authorities to build a poor-house and offer relief therein. They were further entitled to contract with persons for maintaining and employing the poor and taking the benefit of their labour and service.

An Act of 1796 repealed so much of this as prohibited relief being given to poor persons in their own houses, and justices were empowered to order relief to any industrious poor person who is thereupon entitled 'to ask and receive such relief at his or her own house,' and the overseers are bound to obey such order.

We have not space to set out all the disastrous consequences of this policy. In thirty years the dependent population, called into existence by the facilities of relief, brought the country to the verge of ruin. The evils were so glaring that it was possible for a popularly elected House of Commons to pass in 1834 the stringent reforms of the New Poor Law. The Act of 1834 may be said to bring us to the modern era, and we propose later on to say something on the present aspects of the question.

We have endeavoured to trace the causes which in England produced an inequality of property. In the earliest stages of human society life is from hand to mouth, and precarious to all men. There is an equality, not of wealth but of poverty. The increased comfort and security of civilised life are based on the institution of property, and, rightly or wrongly, on the institution of *private* property. Causes connected with, or at least accentuated by, difficulties arising out of a tribal or communistic tenure of land produced the inequalities of the feudal system. Classes were excluded from participation in the advantages of private property, and the social instincts which grow from it. Classes have continued to live under primitive conditions, as far at least as this important element in their lives is concerned. That instinct of property which tends to limit population to the existing development of local or national resources has, of course, had little potency among classes which have no property. The standard of living to which they were willing to bring up their children was a mere maintenance dependent on daily labour. The possession of property was not an item in the standard of living which they strove to maintain. A redundancy of a labouring population was a natural result. Improvements in agriculture, trade, and manufacture absorbed, with only occasional crises, the labour of a rapidly increasing population. So far society proceeded on an economic or individualistic basis. The lower strata, it is true, had been permitted to avail themselves but little of the advantages which the higher civilisation gave. They lived from hand to mouth, a life of toil, but yet of independence. Misfortune, such as old age, sickness, or accident, a check in the advance of trade, a change in the methods of production, a fluctuation of a foreign market, was sufficient to render many of them destitute. A socialistic poor law became necessary. The wholesome principle (the foundation-stone of individualistic society), that each man must find an economic maintenance for himself and family, is abandoned. We have traced very briefly the growing facilities for obtaining a pauper and uneconomic maintenance which humanitarianism put within the reach of the poor. If the instinct of property leads men to measure their responsibilities against their possessions, the instinct of pauperism has also an analogous effect in an opposite direction. In those evil days a poor man calculated unconsciously that the State would provide for him in every contingency. Responsibilities were lightly incurred: the larger the family the more liberal the relief. Employers took advantage of the law and paid wages out of the rates, and reduced the whole labouring class to the condition of slaves.

Worst of all, it led away the attention of the

working class of the country from the direction in which a true solution was to be found, and to the present day it is to be feared their attention, and that of those who wish them well, still at times wanders from the point.

Instincts arising out of the possession of property have been found able to adjust population to the maintenance provided for it. It may be that these instincts can be acquired in other ways. This, however, is clear, that it is only when these instincts permeate the motives and conduct of individuals that the desired consummation is to be found. It is inconceivable that the State can ever contend successfully with the difficulties of a society in which individuals are at liberty to incur all responsibilities, relying with a light heart on the guarantee of the State. Yet this was the frame of mind in which our working population had been bred. Under these fatal delusions the country was called on to meet the momentous changes produced by the invention of machinery and the industrial revolution of the eighteenth century.

CHAPTER VIII

THE INDUSTRIAL REVOLUTION OF THE EIGHTEENTH CENTURY

THE next division of our subject is concerned with the period of the industrial revolution which took place during the latter half of the eighteenth century. The population of England and Wales in 1700 is estimated at 5,000,000. In 1750 it had risen to 6,000,000. In the second half of the century the increase was much more rapid. In 1801 the population was about 9,000,000—an increase of fifty per cent. In the first fifty years of this century the population shows an increase of 100 per cent., and had risen from 9,000,000 to 18,000,000.

This growth of population corresponds with the growth of trade.

This increase of population and trade has taken place principally in the north and midland counties of England.

The density of population per square mile

In 1881 in Lancashire was	1,813	In 1881 in Warwick was .	825
,, 1750 ,, ,, ,,	156	,, 1750 ,, ,, ,,	159
,, 1881 ,, Staffordshire ,,	862	,, 1881 ,, the West Riding of Yorkshire was	815
,, 1750 ,, ,, ,,	140	,, 1750 ,, ,, ,,	141
,, 1881 ,, Durham ,,	891		
,, 1750 ,, ,, ,,	138		

This increase has arisen from the creation of an urban population. The size of our towns has enormously increased, especially the great towns of the north. Liverpool in 1760 had an estimated population of between 30,000 and 40,000, Manchester was perhaps a little larger. In 1881 Liverpool contained 552,000, Manchester 393,000.

This extraordinary growth of population bears evidence to the changes brought about by the industrial revolution.

At the last census it appeared that 66·6 per cent. of the population lived in towns; the rural population was 33·3 per cent.

Gregory King, a political arithmetician, writing about the time of the Revolution of 1688, considered that of an estimated population of 5,500,000, 4,100,000 lived in hamlets and villages. The town population was 1,400,000. Artisans and handicraftsmen he numbers at 240,000 only. Labourers, cottagers and paupers he reckons at 2,575,000. His figures must, of course, be received with caution; there is no reason to doubt, however, that they represent in a general way the relative proportion of the rural and urban population.

Arthur Young (1769) considered that in flourishing countries like England one half of the nation was to be found in towns. He reckons the population at 8,500,000.

Farmers, their labourers, &c.	2,800,000
Manufacturers	3,000,000
Landlords, dependents, miners, fishermen, &c.	800,000
Commercial class	700,000
Non-industrious poor	500,000
Clergy and lawyers	200,000
Civil Service, Army, Navy, &c.	500,000
	8,500,000

In 1688 the rural population was 3 to 1 as compared with the urban population.

In 1769 it was about equal.

In 1881 the town population was double that of the country.

Previous to 1760 the common field cultivation still obtained. Even the best land under this form of cultivation was miserably farmed.

In Arthur Young's verdict never more miserable crops were seen—the whole system absolutely beneath contempt. This is very much what might have been expected. The common field system meant unscientific farming, enormous loss of time to those engaged in the industry, never-ending quarrels.

The history of the improvement of agricultural science goes side by side with the history of enclosures. The question of commonage has been mixed up with many considerations. With the equity of the way in which enclosures were carried out we have nothing here to do; it is admitted that the interests of the poorer classes were not sufficiently considered. The transference of common land into private individual property is in itself an unmixed good. The system of commonage was of little benefit to anyone, if we may believe the testimony of Arthur Young and other competent observers.

Not only the cottager, but the neighbouring farmer and landowner, had a right to commonage, and these last take especial care, says A. Young, by means of their flocks, to starve every animal the poor people can think of keeping.

Commonage also was frequently very far distant, and much time and labour were wasted in going to and fro. For the reasons given it was impossible for a poor man, who had no fields of his own, to carry on a profitable industry by means of the common.

The existence of the common, however, frequently had this effect: that the interest of the labourer was divided between his commonage and his work, and there was a tendency for him to rely on his share in the common for a livelihood, which it could not afford, and where it was impossible for him to be successful. Too often, therefore, there must have been reason in the frequent complaint that commonage encouraged laziness and pauperism.

In some cases, the right of commonage was commuted for an allotment contiguous to the cottage. This arrangement, in Arthur Young's opinion, was generally beneficial. At Folkingham, in Lincolnshire, at least three acres had been allotted, and the people were, he thinks, 'much better labourers for it.' Arthur Young is the inventor of the phrase, the 'magic of property.' Such facts as the foregoing make us feel that the term is no exaggerated eulogy on property as an elevating influence on the habits and status of labour. There is, however, a converse truth which is not so familiar to us, namely, that commonage in land, and in all other things, has only a deadening and distracting effect on the character of an industrial population.

The farmer and landlord class was not favourable to this allotment system; it made the labourer too independent.

> It is clear (says a contemporary writer) that any cottager who has two or three acres of land, keeps a cow and two or three hogs, and grows plenty of potatoes, is not much necessitated to work for others. If every labourer could be so accommodated, famine would inevitably be the consequence in a short space of time.

Arthur Young takes a more liberal view of the situation. 'It is impossible to speak too highly in praise of the cottage system of Lincolnshire, where land, gardens, cows, and pigs are so general in the hands of the poor. Wherever this system is found poor rates are low.'

While it is the opinion of Sir F. Eden, Arthur

Young, and other competent observers, that the advantages of commonage were more apparent than real, at the same time the modern popular view has ground of justification. Undoubtedly the appropriation of the common was carried out on very inequitable terms. The last chance of the labourer of creeping into freedom by means of property now vanished. The last share of the community of which his predecessors had been a part, was enclosed, and his interests too often neglected. His only chance of attaining freedom and property lay, for the future, in a careful husbandry of his wages. But here, alas, the mistaken policy of the times again doomed him to disappointment.

The increase of enclosures might have been expected to increase the demand for agricultural labour. This probably was the case, but wages did not depend on economical laws, but on the regulations of quarter sessions and the poor law allowance. The farmers and landowners used the rates as a means of indemnifying the labourers whom they underpaid. The able-bodied man without encumbrances received the lowest wage that would keep him, or, more often, he was left without employment altogether. The parish authorities obliged the farmer to employ the labourer with children, and, in aid of his wages, an allowance was paid out of the rates for each child.

Thus the bounty-raised population increased out of all proportion to the economical situation. The labourer's position was a very hopeless one. He gained nothing by limiting his responsibilities. Early marriages and large families were encouraged by the rates. The farmers wanted cheap labour and Pitt wanted soldiers for his French war. 'Let us make,' he said, 'relief, in cases where there are a number of children, a matter of right and honour, instead of a ground for opprobrium and contempt.'

Local authorities acted on the advice of the great minister. The bounty thus set on the production of an unprovided-for population produced its effect, and completed the degradation of the labouring population. The possibility of acquiring freedom and property altogether vanished from the horizon of his hopes.

The overflow of this population went into the towns, and formed the nucleus of the new industrial classes of society. Thus was a population provided, ready to be employed, ready to increase and multiply, in the north and in the towns at the bidding of industrial enterprise.

We return for a moment to another aspect of the agricultural situation. The disappearance of the yeomanry, an event generally assigned to the beginning and middle of the eighteenth century, is a matter to which much attention has been given.

Gregory King puts the freeholders 'of the lesser sort' of England at the end of the seventeenth century at 120,000 families.

In the last quarter of the eighteenth century A. Young talked of the entire disappearance of the small freeholder.

Many causes may be set out as contributing to this result.

Previous to the middle of the eighteenth century the country farm house was still the scene of many domestic industries. Events were making a greater division of labour necessary. The small yeoman relied for his maintenance, not only on his farm, but on the industry of spinning and weaving, dyeing and bleaching. These were now to be more profitably carried on in towns, or by means of water power, and later by steam power. The yeoman had to choose which industry he would follow. He could find a ready sale for his interest in the land. Land was the foundation of political power. Rich merchants, and neighbouring landowners were ever on the lookout for adding to their acres. Land, even as now, was not the best investment for a poor man. Taxes and poor rates were enormous, while the new industries had as yet escaped the meshes of the tax collector. Many of the yeomen and small proprietor class no doubt left the land and became captains of industry in the new era which was just dawning. It is stated by some authorities that yeomen were still numerous at the end of last century. If this is so, it would bring the yeoman down to the period of the rise of scientific agriculture. The less adventurous spirits clung to their land ; if careful and thrifty, they added field to field, and budded into squires. The picture of the yeoman so well known in fiction, proud, ignorant, and prejudiced, is probably not far from the truth. He neglected, partly from prudence, partly from prejudice, methods of improved farming, till it was too late ; or, he embarked on them without due knowledge, he borrowed money and got into difficulties, and was only too glad to sell his land at a good price to some rich tradesman anxious to acquire status and not remunerative investment. To these causes, or to a combination of them, the yeoman class succumbed. It is probably incorrect to conclude that they necessarily sank into a lower social stratum. The man who, in earlier times, sustained the due succession of the yeoman class, preferred to embark in the freer and more profitable career of trade ; and the enhanced value of land on political and social grounds prevented men becoming purchasers who had their living to make out of it. They knew, at all events, that they could invest their money better elsewhere. An investment in land might pay well, but an investment in trade paid better

We venture to think that more importance than it merits has been attached to this question of the disappearance of the yeomanry. It only means in our view that, for the future, the best energy of the nation was to run in the freer channels of trade; and that, even to this day, this energy has never been diverted back again to the land. Our barbarous and antiquated system of land tenure has never allowed agriculture to have a fair chance. Land is still subject to the inconvenience of limited ownership. Notwithstanding the stream of modern civilisation setting continuously towards individualisation of property, lawyers have, by means of settlements, entails, and other restrictions, continued to make land the object of a species of communistic tenure. By a strange fatality the first attack of socialistic innovators is made on property in land. It is, however, precisely because their views have been followed in the past that the present impotence has come upon agricultural industry. Tardily, and with the avowed object of staving off revolution, legislation has stepped in to arbitrate between some of the conflicting claims, and commissions are gravely sitting to fix the value of land, as quarter sessions used to fix the price of all commodities in the dark ages. As to the necessity of legislative interference in this present dilemma we offer no opinion, we only insist that the present solution is only temporary. The office of statesmanship with regard to land is to free it from the trammels of divided interests, and to allow its value to be decided by ordinary economic laws. There should be no greater necessity for government to fix the price of land than to fix the price of potatoes.

It has become the fashion among the historical school of political economists to argue that legislative interference with economic questions has often been justified by circumstances, and that mediæval statecraft has in this particular been misrepresented and misunderstood by modern economists. In modern times the success of the factory acts has been urged as an instance of the wisdom of refusing to listen to the advice of the older economists. The question will arise again in the course of our enquiry; we cannot venture to offer any absolute and decided opinion on the matter: at present we only remark that the economists will do well to fortify themselves within the general and impregnable principle, that it is safer, better, more conducive to equality in the long run, to leave men to protect themselves in the economic struggle for property and self-preservation. The economic errors of the past have made it impossible for classes of men at certain junctures of history to maintain the struggle. It may, at such crises, be politic to interfere, but such interference should never be regarded as a permanent arrangement. It is a good thing to give a drowning man a life buoy, but it is better still to bring him to shore. The current may carry the man and the buoy out to sea. The shore in matters economic is the safe ground of individual economic independence, and legislative interference is only useful in so far as it ultimately brings society nearer to this goal.

At the juncture, which we are now considering, the backwardness of agricultural science, owing largely to the lethargic influence of a customary system of cultivation, the heavy taxation which the foreign policy of the government laid upon the landowner, drove the enterprise of the nation into a new channel. The progress of its growth, when turned into the free atmosphere of our trade, gives us some indication of what might have been the spirit of enterprise brought to bear upon agriculture but for the depressing influence of a divided tenure, customary cultivation, and inordinate taxation.

Into the new life of industrial enterprise there was a great transference of population, both of the captains and of the hodmen of industry.

The captains were the picked men of the agricultural leaders, who, disgusted with the bucolic apathy of rural life, felt capable of striking out a new line for themselves. The hodmen were the overflow of a population pauperised by an injudicious poor law, and too little accustomed to a wise husbandry of resources.

Such were the two component parts of the population which was now set sliding down the steep gradients of commercial prosperity. This prosperity continued to increase by leaps and bounds, and to absorb the enormous population which grew up in dependence on it. To provide a maintenance for men is to create them. The elder Peel is reported to have said in 1806 :—

> In the cotton trade machinery has given birth to a new population, it has promoted the comforts of the population to such an extent that early marriages have been resorted to and a great increase of numbers has been occasioned by it, and I may say that it has given rise to an additional race of men.

The demand for the labour of this class was so great, and on the whole so constant, that the circumstances of the time seemed to warrant the idea that a population could live and expand itself, trusting always that the morrow would bring employment and wages. The fundamental condition of civilised life was again lost sight of, namely, that civilised man must not depend on each day providing its own maintenance (as do the lower savages and beasts), but on a careful husbandry of each day's gain. To make this possible, civilisation has invented the institution of property. Property, so husbanded, may be used as maintenance or it may be used as capital to assist in the production of fresh gain. On the individual practice of this elementary law of civilised life, the well-being of all human society and its members rests. English social life had been caught and whirled in such a storm of prosperity that there seemed little occasion to practise this careful husbandry. The working classes had thrust on them or adopted a low standard of living. In that standard, security of maintenance by careful husbandry formed no part.

If they fell out of the ranks of industry there was the poor law ready to start them again in the race or to maintain them if they could work no more. There was bound to be a rude reawakening when England's commercial supremacy came to be disputed and when trade ceased to increase by leaps and bounds. Population continued to increase at its old rate, and the demand no longer absorbed the surplus supply of labourers. Men and classes who have nothing to depend on but their willingness to work are bound to suffer. We are already experiencing this difficulty.

Amid all this prosperity a retrograde process was going on with respect to a certain portion of the community. In a rich man's life there is a considerable margin for economic imprudence and excess. He may lead a stormy youth, and blossom into much respectability in old age; but with the poor there is very little margin. A single false step, a loss of character, a tendency towards vagabondism, not in its first appearance altogether unamiable, a difficult temper, and a thousand other venial infirmities and misfortunes, are sufficient to ruin a poor man. For there is below the industrious working class a gulf of vagabondage into which these stragglers fall. From this abyss escape is very difficult: 'vestigia nulla retrorsum.' It is not, we fear, an altogether unpleasant life. Humanitarian sentiment busies itself much about the outcast classes, pities, feeds, and maintains them. Irregular work, three or four days holiday in the week, a bit of criminal adventure, deputations to timid boards of guardians, meetings in Trafalgar Square, a summer holiday in the hop fields, the free meals and shelter given by philanthropists, are incidents in the career of a London outcast which show that his life, though very degraded, is fairly secure and certain, and not altogether without its pastime and pleasure.

The industrious working class is slowly and surely, by means of its careful husbandry, creeping into freedom and property, much as did the servile tenants of the middle ages, described in the happy phrase of Hallam.

The interest of the modern problem is twofold. We have first to consider the outcast class. What is to be done with them? Their existence presses most heavily on the class immediately above them, and their disappearance would enormously improve its prospects. The second point of interest centres round the efforts made by the industrious working class to creep into freedom and property. Much progress has been made, much remains to be done.

CHAPTER IX

THE THEORY OF WAGES

In the foregoing chapters we have endeavoured to show how much interest, in the history of human civilisation, centres round the institution of property. Before attempting to apply our theory to the elucidation of the modern economic situation, it may be convenient to recapitulate some of the arguments that have gone before.

It is a fundamental condition of civilised life, that men must not consume the reward of their labour on the day on which it is earned. Civilisation postulates some certainty of maintenance and survival from day to day. This is assured to men by the practice of careful husbandry of resources, but even this would be of no avail, if the institution of property did not guarantee to the husbandman the enjoyment of his savings. Property, therefore, is a main condition of survival in civilised society. Religion and custom have assigned to it a dignity in proportion to its importance.

Further, not only is property a condition of

survival, but it marks out for men a series of elementary responsibilities, if they would live according to the rules of civilised life.

(1) Individually, each man's survival depends on his own careful husbandry and thrift.

(2) Socially, also, man must regulate his numbers, and the disposition of his numbers, proportionately to property and to the economic surroundings of the time. A rapidly increasing population may be an unmixed advantage in America, but it is no advantage here in England, if the new growth has not the means to transport itself to places where it is wanted. This disposition and regulation of the increase of population is an elementary responsibility, the bearings of which man can best perceive when he recognises the fact that his own individual existence cannot be purely from hand to mouth, purely proletariate. The peasant proprietor, individually secure in the possession of land, gauges, with comparative ease, the capacity of his land to carry its population. A peasant proprietary is notoriously a population which increases slowly. In other more complicated industries calculation has been more difficult. We have endeavoured to trace the history of the divorce between property and labour, and to show that the instincts which property engenders are even more important for our social well-being than property itself.

We think it is established that these elementary responsibilities, (1) self protection, (2) prudent expansion of the numbers of the population, cannot be deputed by the individual to the state or to any collectivist society.

Human society is an evolution as much as is the animal creation. That wonderful web, which we term human society, would have been pieced together more deftly and more equally if more regard had been paid to the natural and inherited power of individual organisms to fit themselves to their place in the economy of nature. In our survey we have seen illustration of this truth. A collectivist tenure of land led to slavery, villenage, and the feudal system. A train of similar errors, never corrected and never understood, brought us at last to our present industrial system. In the chaos which has invaded mortal affairs many collectivist attempts have been made to repair the errors of the collectivism of the past.

The mediæval trade gild system had some temporary advantages, we have seen its decay into close and useless corporations. It is usual at the present day to utter triumphant pæans over the operation of the factory laws and over the successes of trades' unions. Are we again to be doomed to disappointment? We are not prepared to argue that legislation and collectivist associations are not often necessary and productive of temporary good. We conceive, however, that there is a danger of placing too much reliance on their efficacy, and that it is essential to recognise that they are only good in so far as they give to the individual room to breathe, and a chance of regaining the self-assertive powers which disuse has atrophied. These are *à priori* suspicions which seem to us to fall on modern collectivist attempts to advance the interests of the working classes; it should therefore be our business to watch very closely for germs of degeneration and decay, as well as to examine the limits within which their influence may be productive of good.

To one other point we desire to recall the attention of the reader. In the first chapter we endeavoured to show that most property consisted in more or less developed opportunities for remunerative labour.

The problem of modern economic life is to remove the apparent antagonism which exists between the owners of these remunerative opportunities and those whom they hire to apply their labour thereto, in other words, between capital and labour. Can this reconciliation take place by any other means than by a wider distribution of ownership in the productive apparatus of the country?

A preliminary question has to be settled. Is it possible that a class, entirely dependent on wagedom, can ever possess that assured and comfortable maintenance which civilised ideas lead us to wish?

We have already indicated on *à priori* grounds that it is not possible for classes who have neither property nor the instincts which belong to it to protect themselves, and to regulate the increase of their families, in such a way as to enjoy fully the security of civilised life.

A completer answer can be given if we consider recent theories of wages. It will be interesting to see how far economic speculation bears out the theory which we have propounded as based on the principle of evolution.

In Ricardo's opinion, the progress of society involves a rise of rent, a fall in interest and profit, and a stationary state of wages at or about the level which insures to the labourer a bare maintenance and nothing more. This is the natural rate of wages. If wages rise owing to an increased demand, then population will increase, and wages will fall again to their old level. Wages cannot fall permanently below subsistence, as an increased death rate and restriction of marriages will before long restore the balance. Such is the iron law of wages adopted by socialist writers like Marx and Lassalle, and which in their opinion justifies revolution.

This theory is adopted by Mr. J. S. Mill, with

the important qualification that the level of subsistence is an elastic term.

Ricardo is a writer who takes little pains to enlist sympathy for his views. He is, as he has told us, an elucidator of principles. A doctrine is true or it is false, that is his concern; whether the public finds truth palatable or not, is a question to which he is very indifferent. The modern economist is very anxious to make his science more agreeable to popular aspirations. It is often said that Ricardo's logical and mathematical method has raised a cloud of prejudice against the study of political economy. This may be so, but we question if the modern spirit is more scientific. This point of the variable standard of living by no means escaped the observation of Ricardo, as is often asserted.

> It is not to be understood (he says) that the natural price of labour, estimated even in food and necessaries, is absolutely fixed and constant. It varies at different times in the same country, and very materially differs in different countries. It essentially depends on the habits and customs of the people.[1]

In Mill's hands this qualification is enlarged upon, and becomes the familiar doctrine of the standard of living. Labourers will not always use an increase of wages for the purpose of procreating and maintaining more children. They may use

[1] *Principles of Pol. Ec.*, ed. 1821, cap. v. p. 91.

such increase as an opportunity for adopting a higher standard of living, and the increase of wages has then a chance of remaining permanent. This is a more cheerful view than that attributed to Ricardo. According to this theory demand and supply are still the potent influences, but as far as the supply is concerned it is a good deal under the control of labourers themselves. Ricardo evidently did not think this control was likely to be very effective. Mill, however, assigns to it a very important place in his theory of wages. If labourers are careful and will limit the supply, their position will improve.

The other side of the equation, viz. the demand for labour, depended, according to Mill and the earlier economists, on the amount of the 'wage fund.' He supposes that there is

> at any given instant a sum of wealth which is unconditionally devoted to the payment of the wages of labour . . . it is a predetermined amount. . . . So that the sum to be divided being fixed, the wages of each solely depends on the divisor, the number of the participants.

This view is adopted by Mr. Fawcett, in his statement of the 'Economic Position of the English Labourer,' and generally the theory held the field till quite a recent date.

Although some of Mill's reasons for attributing importance to the Standard of Living are perhaps fallacies, it still evidently has a very important influence both on the amount and on the quality of the supply of labour, and these two points must always be taken into account in any consideration of the question.

But with regard to the existence of a wage fund which occasions the demand for labour, it was admitted by Mr. Mill himself before his death that his view was untenable.

The wage fund theory is erroneous, or merely a truism. It is a truism to say that the amount of wages paid to labourers is a definite sum. But it is entirely erroneous to assume that the wage fund has anything to do except incidentally with accumulations of capital antecedently gathered together. The demand for labour depends on the demand which exists for the products which labour helps to make. The demand for future produce is the true regulator of the demand for labour. In a developed state of credit and commerce, wages are advanced out of capital before the desired product is finished and ready for the market, but this is accidental and not essential to the transaction. In early civilisation, and even now in the Western States of America, wages are paid at the end of the harvest, when the product of the harvest has been sold.

Again, there is undoubtedly a tendency for wages to fall when the number of labourers is in excess of the demand for their services. But this is a view of the subject which requires to be stated with many qualifications. If all labourers were equally competent, the proposition of Mr. Mill that, the sum to be divided being fixed, the wages of each solely depends on the divisor, namely, the number of the participators, might perhaps be true, but even then it is doubtful whether competition so complete has any place in practical life. At all events, at the present day wages are not lowered in order to give employment to the unemployed. Workmen have combined to keep up the rate of wages, and, what is perhaps more important, trades and handicrafts are now so specialised that unemployed labourers rarely have sufficient skill to replace even at lower wages the skilled artisan who commands a high wage. Wages often continue high even when there are a large number of workmen unemployed. The most skilled are employed regularly and at good wages. The presence of the unemployed does not, in most trades, lower wages or ensure a division among all the operatives of the total sum of wages paid in the trade.

Many critics have taken part in demolishing Mr. Mill's theory of wages. The view which is now most generally received is that of Prof. F. Walker.

All the persons who combine to produce a commodity have to obtain their reward out of the commodity in question. The ultimate paymaster of all is the consumer. Economical transactions are much complicated by considerations of credit and by the fact that the consumer has delegated his functions to his agent, the employer. The consumer in each case pays for the services of those who have produced his commodity. It is merely accidental that, as a rule, he pays it to the organiser of labour.

The question to be answered is: In what proportion will the price paid by the consumer be shared among the various persons who have combined to satisfy his wants?

First, the consumer will not give more than he can help, and each party to the transaction will imitate this example. Each will give as much of his service as will enable the transaction to take place, and no more. The price of a commodity will be divided into rent, interest, profit, and wages. Rent is fixed, Mr. Walker maintains, by the formula of Ricardo. The best or most convenient land is occupied first; when population increases the land so occupied is insufficient to meet the wants of the community. The next convenient land is then taken into use. The occupiers of the first land will find that their land has a value over and above the value of the less convenient land. The yearly value of this advantage is a year's rent. The worst land occupied will not pay any rent; it may of course be joined to good land, and nominally a tenant may be found to pay rent for it, but theoretically speaking the worst land will be rent free. The consumer then, on every occasion when he makes a purchase, must pay a price sufficient to reward the person who supplies the land involved in the transaction. In buying a bit of bread a proportionate sum is devoted to pay the rent of the field where the corn is grown, of the mill where the flour is ground, and of the shop where the bread is baked.

Next, the consumer must pay interest to the man who provides the use of the machinery and stock of trade, the convenience of ready money, and generally the facilities of capital.

Capital is generally reckoned in money, the medium of exchange; there is no doubt, therefore, with the consumer what he is paying for. The rate of interest for different risks becomes tolerably well known and understood. If interest rules high in a particular trade capital is attracted to it, and the consumer, or the employer acting on his behalf, being on the look-out for advantage, avails himself of the state of the market and reduces the rate of interest. If the rate is put too low, capital is withdrawn to more eligible investments and the balance is adjusted.

Thirdly, profit must be paid to the man who organises the satisfaction of the consumer's wants. The employer is from a point of view the agent of the consumer. In the consumer's interest the employer or organiser busies himself to find a landlord to supply a suitable bit of land, a capitalist to supply the machinery and capital (in some instances he is his own capitalist). Next he seeks for a suitable staff of workmen; he directs their labour, and is responsible to a large extent in his own pocket for the success of his management. He has to take care to produce the proper article, in the proper quantities, and at the proper place and season, and he has to please the consumer with novelties. Naturally, the competence of employers varies enormously. Consumers require a certain supply, and it is the business of the employers to produce this. In modern commerce the demand of the consumer is, as a rule, pretty fully supplied. The incompetent employer comes into a full market with goods that have been produced under disadvantageous circumstances. He has hired an inconvenient bit of land, his credit is bad, and he works with insufficient capital, or he has sunk money in unnecessary plant; he hires workmen like himself, who do not understand their business, he produces goods indifferent in quality, too great in quantity, takes them to a wrong market, and at an unseasonable time. Naturally, the consumer will not be able to recompense highly an employer who commits all or some of these faults. If the supply of the article in question is far short of the demand he may escape without serious loss, but in modern commerce such an event must be rare, and in most cases employers of this kind become bankrupt in course of time. Commodities are thus produced at very varying cost. That which in price and quality is best suited to meet the demand is absorbed most readily. These are the goods produced by the competent employer who understands his market. The production of the less competent employer is taken into consumption less willingly. It is, however, the cost of his production which regulates the price of the article.

To illustrate this by an instance, let us represent the production in any given trade by the number 12. There is effective demand, let us say, from the consumers of the country for 10. The number 2 then will represent the bankrupt stock of the trade, which can only be got into consumption by selling at a loss, or by tempting bargain-hunters to buy things which they do not really require. The same manufacturer, if he is to remain solvent, will not continue the production of stock that can only be forced by artifice on the consumer. There is, however, in every trade an average amount of such production. It is impossible to draw the line with accuracy between this class of goods and the next which we now describe. We have said there is effective demand for 10. Of this 10, let us suppose that 3 are produced under conditions which barely pay the various parties concerned in the production. This state of things proceeds from incompetence of a less marked character than that which distinguishes the bankrupt producer. There is an effective demand for these goods represented in our illustration by the number 3. They have to compete, however, with 2, and their production is barely remunerative. Goods represented by the balance 7 are produced under conditions in varying degrees superior to the conditions under which 3 are produced.

The superiority of the conditions results in a saving of cost, and proceeds from more efficient management, better machinery, more skilful labour, greater knowledge of markets and times and seasons. There is, *ex hypothesi*, a steady and effective demand for 10, and consumers are able and willing to pay the price which will bring 10 into the market. This price, obviously, is regulated by the cost of production of the 3, not of the 7, and the producers who make the 7 will sell at the same price as the 3, and the larger margin over cost of production will be retained by them as profit. It is true that, owing to competition, there is a tendency to drive down the incompetent producer below the remunerative line from the 3 to the 2. This is mainly brought about by class 7 increasing their output; but at a point, of course, the less competent part of class 7 will find itself engaged in unremunerative production. When the producers of 7 have increased their output to 10, they will have supplied the effective demand, and the number 3 will still represent the production which is relatively least competent, least remunerative, and most costly.[1]

The least competent suppliers of the effective demand of the market regulate the price, but they profit little or nothing by selling their goods. The more competent employer sells the same class of goods at the same price as his incompetent rival. He has of course his partners to reckon with, but as far as the saving is the result of his competence, and not due to advantages of land, capital or labour, he nets the difference in cost of production as his own profit. In a well ordered state of trade there would be a reasonable number of employers all of whom had some capabilities for industrial command, the incompetent would be unable to get credit, and would be obliged to enrol themselves as labourers in the ranks. At the present time it is to be feared that there are too many incompetent organisers in the field. The consumer gets the advantage of an 'enormous sacrifice,' but much discredit and suffering is caused to a wide circle of other persons concerned.[2]

[1] For a fuller discussion of this point see Mill, *Pol. Ec.*, p. 291, people's ed.

[2] Under cover of a foot-note we hazard a pious opinion that the

One mark of the incompetent employer is his employment of under-paid labour. Under-paid labour is always dear. Again, it is the incompetent, ill-equipped employer who sets manual labour to work in unequal competition with machinery, who employs the sweater to manage his sub-contracts because he cannot afford a factory and proper machinery, who is indifferent as to the irregular

State, by lending its machinery for the recovery of debts, is party to a system which keeps the incompetent employer from extinction. The State guarantees that if a debtor is solvent he shall be compelled to pay. The law operates very much in the same way as the law of distraint in England, and the law of hypothec in Scotland. It makes manufacturers and others more inclined to give credit than they otherwise would be. It is often argued in Scotland that the old law of hypothec enabled small farmers without capital to obtain the lease of a farm. This is perfectly true, but it is a question if good farming; and the liberal application of capital to farming was encouraged thereby. Under cover of the State guarantee for the legal enforcement of debts, incompetent employers, that is, employers without sufficient capital, get credit and are enabled to start in business in a way they would never succeed in doing if creditors knew that debts could not be enforced at law. Some curtailment in the State guarantee of business contracts would do much to reduce to more moderate proportions one of the evils of modern times, namely, gambling in the stock and produce markets. The risk of having transactions with gambling customers would considerably reduce such business if the parties concerned knew that contracts could not be enforced. The risks of gambling would be so enormous if performance of agreements depended solely on commercial honesty, that it is difficult to conceive how people could venture to buy and sell except for the legitimate uses of their business. The men and firms which deal largely in market gambling are not, as a rule, those with whom their fellow tradesmen would enter into time bargains if these could not legally be enforced. Such a change would do more to rid commerce of dishonest traders than all the bankruptcy laws that ever were devised.

employment given to his hands, either because he is incapable or because he has no machinery which he is in economy bound to keep going all the year round.

The rule of profit then is not very different, *mutatis mutandis*, to the rule of rent. The worst land which pays for cultivation can claim no rent. Superior land can claim a rent in proportion to its superiority. Similarly, there is a class of employers who only pay their way and make no profit. The more competent employer will gain such profit as his competence can save for him. Thus, according to Professor Walker, rent, interest and profit are fixed by positive reasons, and the residual share of the price of the product will go to the labourer as wages. It has been objected by Mr. Walker's critics, that this statement is a mere truism and adds nothing to our knowledge. In the last edition of his 'Political Economy' Mr. Walker gives his answer. The objectors should refute the account he has given of rent, interest and profit; it will then be open to them to reject his theory that the wage-earner is the residual claimant, and receives the benefit of all that is left after the other claimants are satisfied. Professor Walker then proceeds to illustrate the operation of the rule (paragraph 330 *et seq.*). As we understand it, his illustration is as follows. In a given trade production suddenly

[1] P. 253, *Pol. Ec.*, 1887.

becomes more efficient by reason of an 'improvement in the industrial quality of the labouring class.' There is nothing in this fact to cause rent to increase, 'there is no greater demand made on land; hence cultivation is not pushed down to inferior soils,' and rents are not enhanced. Nor is there anything in this to cause an increase of interest. Incidentally more machinery may be required, but the skilful workman as a rule requires fewer tools and also is more careful in his management of machinery, and, more probably than not, enables production to be carried on with a smaller outlay on plant.

Nor does an improvement in the industrial quality of workmen make a greater demand for skilful employers. On the contrary, the standard of business ability in the employing class would be raised. The more incompetent employers would be driven out, 'the lower limit of production in this respect would be raised, and the aggregate amount realised as profits would be reduced.' So far Professor Walker's theory appears unassailable. We must say, however, with all deference, that though it sets out very clearly the relation of rent, interest, profit and wages, and of the partnership which unites in productive operations, it does not explain the relation of the consumer to the wage-earner. Or again, while it makes it clear that wage-earners are probably the largest gainers in the improvement of productive methods, it does not explain to us the nature of the minimum and maximum which the consumer will pay for the services of the workmen employed.

It would appear, to adopt Mr. Walker's own phrase, that the consumer in a sense becomes a rival 'residual claimant.' Under certain circumstances the advantage of improved methods of production may be appropriated entirely by the consumer. Little or no rise in wages will take place, but the consumer will buy his goods cheaper. A necessary corollary is added to Mr. Walker's theory by the late Mr. Stanley Jevons, with whom Mr. Walker believed himself to be in agreement. He gives the following account of this aspect of the question.[1]

An increase of production resulting from causes other than those which enhance the claim of rent, interest, and profit, is to the advantage of labour and will make wages rise. Mr. Jevons adds this important qualification :—

Unless, indeed, the price of produce has fallen, and the public, as consumers, have the benefit. Whether this latter result will follow or not depends upon the number of labourers who are fitted for the work. Where much skill and education is required, extensive competition will be impossible, and a permanently high rate of wages will exist. But if only *common labour* is requisite the price of

[1] *Theory of Political Economy*, p. 259.

the goods cannot be maintained, and the public will have the advantage of cheaper supplies.

The skilled artisan will command a price representing the advantage which he confers on the partnership by reason of his skill being greater than that of the commonest labourer engaged in satisfying the consumer's demand. The price paid for every commodity in the consumer's market is regulated by the cost price of that portion of the commodity which is produced under conditions the most disadvantageous warranted by the demand of the market. Now, one of these disadvantageous conditions is undoubtedly the necessity of employing less competent workmen. What rate of wages is the consumer able to pay to the less competent workman? This appears to us to be a key of the situation. The answer will fix the minimum rate of wages. The skilful artisan will receive an addition to the minimum rate in proportion to his skill.

We confess that, with regard to common labour, we do not see any escape from the proposition of Ricardo, namely, that the minimum rate for the lowest class of labour must be a bare maintenance at the standard of living in vogue among the working class. Although these are the general features of the situation, there are one or two minor considerations which either escaped or appeared trivial to the mathematical mind of Ricardo. One is that the standard of living may be made to include most of the comforts which a working population can reasonably want. We are far from having reached that ideal, but there may be no inherent impossibility in it. Secondly, intelligent competition is not impossible. Trade-unionism has not operated largely in the lower scale of labour, but undoubtedly it has been an effective weapon for the protection of working-class interests; but its want of universality has of necessity curtailed its usefulness. The natural trade-union of the family would be much more effective if our working classes understood more clearly the economic necessities of their position. The family has some power to keep its under-paid members out of the market. By adopting more thrifty habits, and by aiming at higher ideals, in fact, by 'competing intelligently,' the lowest stratum of our working population may do much to improve their position; but as far as we can see it must be admitted that the rate of their wages depends almost entirely on questions of demand and supply.

Even if the whole of our labouring population becomes skilful, the wages of the least skilful will always be fixed at the sum which will provide them with the current standard of living. At a lower rate than this they will not work, and their friends and families will support them in a struggle to maintain that standard. Higher wages, it may further be added, and a more intelligent use of them, will much increase effective demand for commodities. This increasing demand for commodities will naturally absorb much of the surplus supply of labour. Such a state of things is a moderate ideal, and will satisfy many. There is, however, in this intelligent application of competition in his own interest, nothing which guarantees to every labourer a right of continuous employment.

Such, however, is the highest ideal which the facts of the case allow us to form as to the future prospects of a population relying on the present conditions of wagedom. Before proceeding to ask whether this is all that civilisation is able to give us, it is necessary to point out that much that is satisfactory even in this ideal depends not on wagedom alone, but on careful thrift and husbandry in the saving and spending of wages.

To compete intelligently a man must not spend his wages on the day he earns them ; if he does so he is the prey of the first grasping employer that he meets. Again, not only he but his family and his class must aid him by their thrift in keeping a good market for his labour. Further, when he comes to spend his wages he must do so intelligently, in the encouragement of industries that employ labour, not in drink or unproductive pleasures, or by rushing into an early and prolific marriage. It should be remembered in this connection that the labouring classes are the largest consumers of commodities, and that with a more thrifty expenditure their consumption of the products of labour might be largely increased.

While admitting that these considerations warrant us in taking a hopeful view of the future of the labouring classes, we are not disposed to rest content with any ideal which bases their prosperity on a system of wage-earning only. The precarious position of a population relying for its maintenance on labour alone, is too obvious. At this stage of civilisation such a state of things is a social anachronism. The labouring population should in some way be enabled to guide itself by, and to control, the opportunities for remunerative labour which exist in the country. The problem of the future is the solution of this difficulty: How is the individualisation of property to be brought about?

The socialist has a rough and ready way. The capital of the country (consisting, as we have seen, in opportunities for remunerative labour) must be 'socialised,' that is to say, it must be managed by the State in the interest of the labouring class. In this way the State will be able to guarantee continuous employment for all men, whatever be their habits of life and standard of living. Such a proposal appears to us to leave out of view all considerations of history and human nature.

Civilisation has been built up by personal thrift,

and depends for its well being on personal prudence and on the power of individuals to adjust themselves to their environment. The proposals of socialism ignore the history of society, and would remove all motive for prudent conduct on the part of individuals. Personal extravagance would entail no inconvenience, and the whole resources of a country would be devoted to maintain, not a high level of comfort, but merely an ever-increasing number of individuals with an ever-decreasing sense of personal responsibility. A promise of maintenance, whether it be offered by the rise of a new industry or by an engagement entered into by the State to provide for all comers, creates a new population. The growth of population in the north of England in response to the growth of trade is a historical fact. The socialist proposes that the State shall guarantee maintenance and eligible employment to a whole nation, quite irrespective of trade considerations. Under such a stimulus population would increase at a rate altogether unprecedented in the annals of the world, and the struggle for existence would begin in grim earnest.

An attack on the system of wagedom has been made from a somewhat unexpected quarter. In a little book published by the Liberty and Property Defence League, Mr. Wordsworth Donisthorpe proposes a scheme for labour capitalisation. Hired labour, argues Mr. Donisthorpe, is a relic of serfdom. To be wholly free the labourer should put himself in a position to bargain for some of the profits of industry. He can do so by capitalising his labour. There is some method in this paradox, though it reads like a proposal for squaring the circle. Mr. Donisthorpe argues as follows :—

> Now it is clear that if instead of accepting wages—letting themselves out for hire by the week or the hour—the workers entered into the venture as capitalists and free men, receiving instead of a fixed wage a certain pre-arranged percentage of the gross produce (a percentage at first based on a calculation of the amount paid in wages over a number of years), the receipts of the hands would vary like the profits of other capitalists, with the success of the venture and the state of trade.

This is all very well, but it is not practical business. Labour is not capital, and cannot be capitalised. As a form of bargain between labour and capital this arrangement would have its advantages, but it is clearly only applicable to a very limited number of industries. Further, there are many circumstances under which a willingness to labour is in no way a valuable commodity. Labour, whether it is digging or piano-playing, is only valuable when it is wanted. The problem is to adjust the number of labourers to the amount of work that is to be done. As far as we can see, this adjustment cannot be brought about by a combination of labourers such as Mr. Donisthorpe suggests. Mr. Donisthorpe proposes that the labourer should offer to go into partnership with the employer; but what is a labourer to do who is told that the employer declines the partnership, or that he is suited with labourers, or, in short, that he will pay wages but will not listen to partnership? Under such circumstances, the labourer must continue in the servile condition of a wage-earner.

We are disposed to agree with Mr. Donisthorpe and with the socialists in saying that the precarious position of the wage-earner is unsatisfactory. The real cause of his servile condition is not his wage-earning, as Mr. Donisthorpe suggests, but the divorce of his class from capital.

A naked proletariate is, economically speaking, an archaic survival from primitive barbarism. On page 126 Mr. Donisthorpe writes, 'I do not propose to discuss the expediency of the institution of private property. I shall assume that it is the most economical means of equitable distribution attainable by man.' This is admirably put. In our view, private property is even more than this. The inoculation of individuals with the instincts of private property supplies the key to the solution of our social difficulties.

Materially speaking, the possession of private property renders a man independent. This is an obvious truism. Morally speaking, it endows him with instincts which will prevent his bringing into the world children whom he cannot support and to whom he cannot give a chance of independent livelihood. To himself it gives habits which preserve him in independence. It solves the antagonism between Labour and Capital. A man who is working for himself as a participator in respect of his capital in the profits of industry finds his toil a labour of love. Even if the capital which he holds is not invested in the trade at which he works, he yet gains out of his possession some insight into economic problems which are now hid from him. Further, it enables him to 'compete intelligently,' to use a phrase of Mr. Walker's. A man who has some savings is not the prey of the first grasping employer whom he meets; not only is he in a position to defend himself by refusing inequitable terms, but he is able to help his fellows in similar efforts and to raise gradually, and on a sure foundation, the whole status of labour.

The feverish enterprise of modern competition is not a distinguishing feature of a state of society in which there exists a wide distribution of property. A peasant proprietary possibly is often narrow, miserly, and too conservative of antiquated methods of cultivation. The large scale of production, whether in agriculture or manufactory, is probably the most efficient. Manufacturing industry is already organised on this large scale, but the limited liability Acts have enabled shares in such undertakings to be held by small capitalists, so that even if the labouring classes are able to push into part ownership of the productive apparatus of the country there is no reason to depart from this system.

To sum up, there are many roads by which the labouring classes may, to use again the expressive phrase of Hallam, creep into freedom and property. There is the obvious course open to him who exercises careful husbandry of his wages. Wages are larger now than they were fifty years ago, and the cost of living is less. There must, therefore, be a larger margin for saving. Saving for a poor man is difficult, but still it must be done. In thrift and saving is the origin of all capital and all property.

Again, successful attempts have been made in co-operative industry. The fatal flaw which has prevented a wider extension of the system is the want of the prompt, decisive, authoritative guidance which is so essential in industrial enterprise.

Mr. Sedley Taylor has much to say in favour of industrial partnerships. Too often these depend solely on the altruism of benevolent employers. The scheme is, therefore, capable of only very limited application. Of the admirable substitute for a private tenure of property provided by the modern expedient of insurance, we shall have something to say in a later chapter. By these and other means the inoculation of the masses with property, and with the instincts of property, is going on. Here if we are not entirely mistaken, the interest of the modern social problem centres. It should be the object of all thinking men to further the process. Too much reliance is placed on collectivist effort, and too little on the necessity of individual independence.

Trades-unions and co-operative societies have to some extent the command of capital. The following suggestion is with deference submitted for the consideration of the managers of these associations, namely, that it might be possible to take advantage of the breaking up of the single capitalist system, which is going on by means of the limited liability Acts, in the interest of the working class. It might be possible to invest some of these funds in well-established industrial undertakings. In our view it would be essential that such investments should not be held permanently by a corporation or trust. The shares so acquired in our national industries should be distributed again among such individual members of the working class as were willing to purchase them on reasonable terms. Such shares might even, by arrangement, be made to confer certain rights of employment.

The problem of the future is becoming clearer, at least, to those who take the trouble to think; but there still exists a vast amount of ignorance and misdirected energy. There are the workmen, who have been deluded by socialistic absurdities. There are the philanthropists, who wish to kick the self-supporting bottom out of society, by degrading every one who is in danger of falling to the level of the out-door pauper and mendicant. There are the careless and thriftless workmen, who insist on paying too large a share of our national drink bill, and who, by this almost wholly unproductive expenditure, starve the domestic industries of the country. Then there come the fair-traders, and the emigration faddists, all directing attention away from the real point of the dilemma, namely, the rescue of our proletariate from its uncertain position by means of the individualisation of property.

CHAPTER X

PRIVATE PROPERTY AND POPULATION

IT appears from the foregoing that the condition of the skilled artisan is in many respects a hopeful one; but it is chiefly hopeful in this, that with only moderate industry, intelligence, and thrift he has every chance of being not only a wage-earner but also a capitalist. At present, unfortunately, he cannot often obtain a share, such as will sweeten his toil, in the business where he is engaged; but other tenures of property have been invented—of these he has availed himself, and so much improved the security of his position. By means of his trade-union he has established an *equitable* right to a share in enhanced profits. Coal-owners object, and object no doubt on sound economical grounds, that wages have nothing to do with profit; still they submit, and submit willingly, to the arbitration of the sliding scale. The miner, through the trade association, has capitalised, not his labour, but his acquiescence to certain terms. The coal-owner accepts the position, and so relieves himself of a great anxiety and uncertainty. In this sense the miners' labour is capitalised, and in return for this the owners agree to increase wages when profits allow of it.[1]

Insurance against sickness and death is another expedient for gaining the security of property. This has been much used by the more intelligent classes of workmen. There is further the old-fashioned plan of saving, much developed and strengthened by an improved system of savings banks and building societies.

With regard to unskilled labour, the outlook is less hopeful. The grosser forms of manual labour can, many of them, be performed more efficiently by means of machinery. There is still an enormous demand for unskilled labour, but it is doubtful if the demand for it expands as fast as the unskilled population increases. Digging is a primæval form of unskilled labour. At the Manchester ship canal steam navvies are at work. Each of these engines is under the control of about ten men, and does the work of eighty men.

The question, therefore, with regard to unskilled labour resolves itself into one of population. Regarding property as being for the most part essentially a right and opportunity for remunerative labour, it becomes apparent that when classes do not regulate the multiplication of the species in proportion to their possession of these opportunities

[1] See Price, *Industrial Peace*, p. 87.

for labour, congestion of population and enforced idleness are occasioned.

A reference to the tables of the Registrar-General shows that while the professional classes marry at the average age of 31, the labouring and artisan class marry at the average age of 24. Further, the same authority tells us that more workmen marry in their 21st year than in any other year of their lives.

The following table is taken from the 49th Annual Report of the Registrar-General, p. viii. It shows that prudence as to incurring the responsibility of marriage varies almost exactly in inverse proportion to the necessity for it.

Average Age of Marriage.

Miners	24·06	These five divisions comprehend the working class. The average age of marriage among the whole class is 24·85.
Textile hands	24·38	
Shoe-makers and tailors	24·92	
Artisans	25·35	
Labourers	25·56	
Commercial clerks		26·25
Shopkeepers, shopmen		26·67
Farmers and sons		29·23
Professional and independent class		31·22

Early marriages mean large families. The rate of infant mortality among the working class is very high, and the evils attending the employment of young married women in factories are very great. A very terrible account of the misery resulting from the enforced toil of married women, is given by Mr. Stanley Jevons in the *Contemporary Review* for January 1882. Notwithstanding this mortality, there can be little doubt that the working class increases much more rapidly than the propertied classes. The distinction now made suggests the true cause. Persons who have property rely on it for maintenance for themselves and for their children, and they regulate their increase according to the measure of their property.[1]

The labouring class is less influenced by these considerations. They live from hand to mouth, and expect their children to do the same. Moreover, in a proletariate community, the sense of profit arising from children's labour does much to counterbalance the sense of parental responsibility, and it becomes clearly the labourer's interest to marry young and have the assistance of his children as soon as possible.

Economists and moralists alike see and point out the evil results of these early marriages, but it is much more difficult to create sufficiently attractive motives for bringing about a different state of things. It becomes therefore necessary to point out, as a matter of great historical importance, that the only known influence which has been potent

[1] Miss Collett, a lady who has written a careful account of the working women of East London for Mr. Booth's volume, *Labour and Life of the People*, remarks that in East London, with few exceptions, all working girls marry; and adds this is not the case in the middle class. What an indifference to the arts of intelligent competition the fact discloses!

to restrain an undue growth of population has been, not the mere desire for property, *but the actual possession of property.* This is not a mere distinction of words. The professional and middle classes of England, and the peasant proprietors of the continent, have not unduly increased in numbers, mainly we affirm because, guided by the instincts of property, they increase their numbers only in proportion to the economic maintenance provided for them. The unpropertied classes have had no such guide, and, as if with a desire to obscure the true situation, an uneconomic maintenance has been provided for the surplus of the labouring population, and a bounty set on the procreation of children by our system of poor law relief.

There are many ways in which men can exist in modern industrial society. (1) Men may rely on property as a guarantee for maintenance, or, as in the case of a peasant proprietor, as a means of finding remunerative employment. (2) They may live by labour only, consuming each day the wages which they earn, expecting always that trade will go on expanding, and that it will absorb every increase of population. (3) They may adopt the habits of parasites, and live on the maintenance provided by the poor law and charity.

Men seem to be capable of living by any one of these expedients. If they adopt the first, it is not until they have satisfied their desire and have become possessed of property, that the magical effect on character becomes apparent. Indeed, until property has been acquired there exist no data for calculation and for the full and intelligent exercise of thrift. On the other hand, if men elect or are forced to live entirely from hand to mouth, the fact has also its influence on character. They propose the same ideal for their children, namely, the life of wagedom and the consumption of each week's wages as it is earned. Property is no part of their standard of living. Again, if men are forced to survive as paupers and mendicants, they endeavour to avoid even the suspicion of having property. All this is a phase of evolution. Instincts, habits, and character naturally adapt themselves to their environment, and to the means of livelihood which exists for each case. In the last two modes of existence there is no object in deferring marriage, nor any acknowledgment of responsibility for the adjustment of population to realised property. These classes look to wagedom or to poor law relief for their support, and this consideration in itself contains no incentive to prudence and thrift. The improbability of an expanding trade being able to absorb all additions to population is too remote a consideration to be operative. On the other hand, a man who relies to some extent on his property knows that he has to divide it among his children, and is more careful.

We maintain, therefore, that it is the actual possession of property and the reliance on it for maintenance which is able to regulate population proportionately to the economic maintenance provided for it.

Let us consider how this principle has acted in the period which we have surveyed. Till the middle of last century England was almost solely an agricultural community, at the present day the aggregation of multitudes in towns for the purposes of industry has enormously enhanced the value of land. Land is a necessary factor in all production of wealth, and, therefore, has naturally and inevitably become an object of desire and so of value. Capital was till the middle of last century largely represented by land, and land is still a very large item in the wealth of our country.

Yet the whole policy of our land laws has tended, not to distribute and render mobile this valuable commodity and the healthful magic which it carries with it, but to tie it up with absurd restrictions and to concentrate its ownership in few hands. We have shown that this impotence of the appropriating instinct with regard to land was due to the force of the counter-influence of communism or socialism. Through all these centuries land has been 'socialised' according to the lights and prevailing influences of the time. The collectivist instinct first had its way in the origination of the village community. This has developed into the feudal system and its barbarous, lethargic, customary system of agriculture, and has entailed on us a load of evils from which we are only beginning to escape.

Yet to-day, with a boldness and enthusiasm which we could wish was devoted to some saner purpose, the socialist is again coming forward with his nostrum, and apparently without any suspicion that we are suffering from evils which his advice has created for us. When property is socialised, it is deprived of more than half its value —it cannot be used and improved with the freedom and experimental ingenuity of private property. But to our mind the strongest argument against socialism is that socialised property carries with it no guidance for individual conduct; and yet on individual conduct depends the proper adjustment of society to the surroundings of the time. Man's well-being depends not entirely on precepts of virtue; to urge a man to thrift, and continence, and a prudent increase of his species is good, but, as history shows, these motives are not operative for long, or on the average, except under certain material conditions. These material conditions consist in a wide distribution of private property, and are a necessary antecedent to all healthy progress and freedom. This point of view has been too much overlooked by all parties in this controversy. The truth about this population question appears to be that it can only be solved *ambulando*, that is to say, by the growth of instincts arising out of the influence of property on character. Without the help of this school of experience exhortations to virtue and continence will have little or no effect.

1. On the one hand, therefore, it is most necessary that the magic influence of property towards prudence and self-restraint should be allowed free play; there is no reason (unless some fresh will o' the wisp is started by collectivist activity) why the artisan class, which is now struggling manfully into independence and property, should not be permeated with this wholesome influence. The fringe of the proletariate would grow narrower, and would gradually disappear before the same solvent forces which destroyed the slavery and serfdom of mediæval society.

2. On the other hand, the tendency downwards towards uneconomic conditions of existence must be carefully restrained. If poor law guardians and enthusiastic philanthropists insist on making eligible provision for all who cannot support themselves in economic independence, it is difficult to see how the rottenness of the foundation on which society then rests can be repaired. The struggle of the poorer classes upwards into independence

and property is hard and arduous, but the process is not made easier by incentives to embrace an existence soothed into dependence by the narcotics of poor law and charitable relief.

Another consideration forces itself on our attention. In the first fifty years of the present century the population of this country was doubled, the rate of increase is now slower. In the United States of America population has doubled itself in twenty-five years. The population of France is at this moment diminishing. Yet certainly in England the balance of advantage, with regard to the condition of the labouring class, as between the early years of the century and now is in favour of the present time. Notwithstanding the increase of population, there is undoubtedly an increase of comfort in the lives of the bulk of the working class. In France and in America as well as in this country, there is destitution in the towns, and there is probably not much to choose between the condition of the poor in a growing and a diminishing population.

It is not a question of population, but a question of adjustment. It is perfectly possible that in a century hence the population of England may be double its present number, yet that the average of contentment, happiness, and comfort may be higher than at present.

Again, adjustment turns largely on different

methods of expenditure. In this country the cost of government and unproductive expenditure on the Army and Navy grow by leaps and bounds. The money so spent is abstracted by various devices of taxation from the industries of the country. Our national habit of extravagance in the matter of strong drink has been much aggravated, if it has not been caused, by Government interference with the mobility of property. By our system of land tenure, the State has destroyed the most natural and legitimate use of savings. Investment in the apparatus of production and in its development is the natural alternative and rival to a wasteful consumption on drink. Being deprived of this alternative men have learnt to indulge in the fancied pleasures of strong drink. The legislature takes advantage of our national weakness which its predecessors have helped to teach us, and raises by indirect taxation an enormous revenue from the drink traffic. Indirect taxation tends to profligate public expenditure. The country does not know exactly what it is paying, and therefore scrutinises the items less closely. In this way the taxpayers of this and other countries continue to support the intolerable and growing cost of national armaments. The chain of causation appears unbroken, one false step necessitates another. If property were more accessible, habits would slowly alter, wages would be more wisely spent, governments would be obliged to rely on direct taxation and to curtail their insane rivalry in warlike expenditure, and population would naturally and automatically be made proportionate to the maintenance provided for it.

An accessible tenure of private property is a postulate to the practice of thrifty, prudent living. The discouragement to thrift and saving by the absence of these conditions has been, and still is, enormous. Land has been socialised to the purposes of feudalism; a due development of this system produced the modern form of industrialism, that is, the employment of capital for production on a large scale. The poor man has not been able to acquire land till, owing to foreign competition, land is comparatively valueless; it is very difficult to apply small savings to industrial production under modern conditions. Trade combinations have been illegal till recent times. Out-door poor law relief removes many of the motives for developing friendly societies and clubs. Considering the history of the subject, it is extraordinary that the working classes have done as much as they have in the way of gaining for themselves security by acquiring tenure of property, and the various substitutes for it which we have described.

The first steps in thrift have been and still are arduous, and in a sense unnatural. They are the first variations from the savage type of life which the principle of heredity and evolution has been able to crystallise into the habits of civilised life. The practice of thrift as a means of survival becomes each generation easier and more natural, and in the course of its practice various new and minor adjustments arise. First men survive by thrift, and as a sort of corollary population gets adjusted to maintenance. For as soon as the advantage and necessity of thrift and property is seen and allowed to prevail, the primitive sexual instincts of the savage are subordinated to a new and more important condition of survival. Again, thrifty living increases and equalises the purchasing power of the community; there is a regular demand for articles of common use, which does not fluctuate with change of fashion. Hence employment is more regular, and even wagedom pure and simple has a better chance of comfortable and continuous maintenance.

The ideal of those who accept these arguments must be the individualisation, not the socialisation of property. A human being is not properly fitted for civilised conditions of life till he has acquired the prudent instincts of self-preservation. These, as far as we can see, can only be acquired through an intimacy, so to speak, with the principle of private property.

The intelligent and successful competition of

the workman with his employer becomes possible when property is widely distributed. If the labouring class were also small capitalists the driving and misery of our present abortive system of competition would cease. The business of production would become a mere healthful recreation rather than a grinding and unremitting toil. Nor would its efficiency be impaired. A high remuneration of labour would give an impulse to the invention of machinery, and with this assistance educated and skilful labour would produce for us better and cheaper commodities than before. And in all this advantage the labourer would share, for in the new era he will be capitalist and consumer as well as the mere hodman of industry.

There has been lately some revival of Malthusian speculations about population. The great importance of the question is obvious enough. We have already indicated our view that there is some confusion of cause and effect in this matter. Population increases most rapidly when the units which compose it are poor. To say to a man, 'Be continent, marry late, and have a small family,' is good advice, but it is not attractive enough to influence his conduct. The object of this continence, namely, the acquisition of property and independence, is not an item in the ideal of certain classes of the community, because it is an ideal from which they have been debarred by the perverse ingenuity of State and socialistic intervention. When, however, poor people have been inoculated with the instinct of property, they have no difficulty in conforming to the Malthusian advice. The Malthusian advice is good, but it cannot be followed with average human nature except with the assistance of a certain material condition, namely, the accessibility of property.

The controversy has turned into a side issue. Persons who know something of the way the poor live are aware that much misery, poverty, and mortality arises from the large families of working people. Moralists also complain of the evils of deferred marriage, and it is asked, is it not possible to combine early marriages with small families? This is a totally different question, and one into which we cannot here conveniently enter. We only insist that the difficulty does not arise in communities where property has a chance of acting as a guiding principle, and it appears to us to be best to leave the solution of it to be found by this material instinct of mankind rather than make it a question of moral casuistry.

Another matter which lies on the confines of the population question has also been discussed. It is asserted that the excessive prudence of the well-to-do in this respect may tend to a deterioration of the race. The reckless and the poor, who to some extent are the unsuccessful, and who in a state of nature would be unable to survive or to rear a progeny, under modern conditions have the most numerous offspring. When they cannot support their children themselves the poor law does it for them. The most numerous survivals are therefore the children of the unfit. There is truth in this view, but the matter is inevitable. The man who has any idea of the responsibilities of civilised life does not breed like a beast. The only escape possible from the danger pointed out is to be found first and mainly by a wider inoculation of the masses with the instinct of property, and secondly by a rigid administration of the poor law. Parents must be held to their responsibilities, and maudlin sentimentalists must be restrained from their mischievous activity by a more wholesome tone of public opinion.

We have space only for a few words on the subject of emigration. We have endeavoured to explain our view of the alleged over-population of this country. The country is over-populated in the sense that the supply of unskilled labour is greater than the demand. This relative over-population is caused by thriftless marriages, and perhaps even more by thriftless expenditure.

In face of these causes producing this relative congestion as fast as it is relieved, what possible good can be obtained from emigration? What we require is to force this residual population to adopt the habits and character of civilised life. We use the terms habit and character in a material, and not in a moral, sense. The issues are obscured by the importation of terms of moral praise and blame. It is deplorable that a man should want a leg, and it is socially deplorable that he should want the instinct of self-preservation according to the rules of civilised life; moral praise or blame are, in both cases, inapplicable.

It is, in our view, useless to send away to other quarters of the globe the residuum of our population, if we do not introduce at the same time some principle of conduct which will prevent the rise of a similar class. Emigration is a palliative, a good and useful palliative, but there is no permanency in the relief which it gives, and if we wish really to get to the root of the matter, and are desirous of discovering and setting out on the true road to reformation, we are wasting our time in considering emigration as a possible restorative of the health of the body politic.

CHAPTER XI

THE MODERN ASPECT OF THE POOR LAW

OUR social instincts, which are perhaps the religious development of a sentiment at first merely gregarious, make us desire a greater amount of equality among all classes of men. It is right that we should wish to see the poorer classes of the country sharing, more largely than they do at present, in the security of maintenance which civilisation ought to give. If it were not for this moralised instinct we might absolve ourselves from all concern in the process of human domestication. We should then regard differences of social condition in human society as the divergences of incipient varieties or species. Such a view is repellent to our humanity; we desire to see human progress, or in a narrower sense national progress, represented by a more or less uniform type of prosperity and comfort. We seek to raise the poorer classes, which, from causes for which the present generation is not responsible, have fallen below the due level of comfort, to a state more consonant with the demands of civilised sentiment.

This is the problem. It is the business of the statesman to discover the law of progress, and to endeavour to give free scope to its operation at those points of our social arrangements where reformation is necessary.

Our argument has been that most of the evils from which we are suffering have been brought about by State interference with the natural ability of each individual organism to adjust itself to its environment. Secondly, the evil has been increased by this very ability of adjustment which, if left to itself, plays so wholesome a part in human affairs. The State has debarred individuals from seeking their natural protection by reliance on the institution of private property. It has thus reduced them to a proletariate condition. Then, in an hour of contrition, as it were, the State has sought to atone for its injustice, and, in place of the economic independence provided by nature, it has offered an uneconomic maintenance through the poor law and other socialistic legislation; and such is the adaptability of life even to degraded conditions of survival that a vast class has pushed in to occupy the maintenance thus artificially provided.

The object of modern statesmanship should be, not to plunge forward into the unlimited slough of social legislation, but cautiously, and with a due regard to existing circumstances, to withdraw these uneconomic conditions of life, and to allow them to be replaced by the healthy vigorous expanding framework of individual right and liberty.

It would take too long, and would require a minuteness of knowledge which the author does not claim to possess, if he were to attempt here to traverse the whole history of socialistic legislation. Such legislation is mainly of two kinds. (1) It is in restraint of the mobility of property as in our land laws, or it prohibits and discourages legitimate attempts at self-protection, by means of insurance and combination. The most glaring and iniquitous instances of these were the old law against workmen's combinations, the old law of settlement, and the discouragement to working class insurance by gratuitous medical and out-door relief. (2) Socialistic legislation maintains below the level of independence a class whose existence is a dead weight on the healthy industries of the country. At every turn the solvent Peter is robbed to pay for the insolvent Paul. In towns the cost of maintaining Paul is added to the rent of Peter's house. A pauper class is created, and the difficulty of housing the working classes in towns is aggravated by the incidence of the poor rate. This parasitic class drags down the level of economic maintenance, which depends, as we have seen, on the standard of comfort adopted by the working class. The provision for it made by the State is too easily accessible. The State, as it were, is made to pay bounty out of the rates of the country for its maintenance and increase.

It will be found that all socialistic legislation partakes of these two characteristics. It is either in restraint of, or in competition with, economic conditions of life. It must be admitted that, at the present time, some classes in the State have a sort of vested interest in the continuance of philanthropic legislation. Such legislation is, it is true, a very feeble protection, but the State has covenanted to give it, people have relied on it, and in justice it can only be withdrawn gradually.

It is proposed in this chapter to deal in some detail with the present system of poor law administration.

It is, it need hardly be said, quite impossible to repeal the poor law, but it is possible to administer it in such a way that it shall no longer be a direct incentive to pauperism.

Many persons are very ignorant as to the state of the law, and as a preliminary to a discussion of the subject it seems desirable to set out as briefly as possible its present administration, more especially as it affects London.

In London, as in most populous places, poor law relief is regulated by the Out-door Relief Regulation Order of 1852. Under this order relief, if it is given outside the workhouse, has to be administered weekly; speaking broadly, the assistance given must be by way of maintenance: the rates may not be employed to set up applicants in business, to pay rent, or to redeem tools.

Guardians may relieve any destitute person who is chargeable to their union by receiving him or her into the workhouse, and they can relieve at their own homes by out-door relief all classes of destitute persons, with the one exception of able-bodied males and their families. These can be relieved outside the workhouse only on condition of the head of the family submitting to a labour test. In the country, under the Out-door Relief Prohibitory Order of 1844, the guardians have not this option, and can only relieve the able-bodied in the house. Both in town and country exception is made in favour of cases of sickness arising in the family of the able-bodied man. The labour test is generally exacted in the labour yard; it consists, as a rule, of stone-breaking or some similar task work, but the discretion of the guardians as to the nature of the work is practically unfettered.

Wayfarers and homeless persons are relieved in the casual wards, and are subject to another set of Acts and Orders, of which the principal are those of 1871 and 1882, the latter known as Pell's Act. The casual poor obviously do not belong to the union in which they apply. The charge of their maintenance is therefore in London put on the Metropolitan Common Poor Fund, which is assessed on the rateable value of all London. A casual pauper is not entitled to discharge himself before nine in the morning of the second day following his admission, nor before he has performed his task. If he has been more than once during the month in a casual ward within the union (and for this purpose London is reckoned as one union), he may be detained to the fourth morning. The authorities have power to allow men to go out earlier than the hour and day named if they appear to be in search of work. The use of this discretion has recently been urged on guardians by circulars from the Local Government Board. It is therefore an entire misrepresentation to say that the stringency of the law is such as to prevent men seeking for work. This special provision for the homeless has created a special class of pauper, and the best authorities are anxious to see the casual ward abolished. The maintenance provided is a very degraded one, but it is safe, and not at all precarious, and many poor creatures are thus tempted to live down to it. The ragged clothes and slouching air of the casual make his employment impossible, and he is bound to the life of a tramp all his days. Such a life has its enjoyments ; he begs and steals a bit, he sleeps in the open in summer, and shares in the fortuitous charity of London and large towns during the winter. One of these casuals recently told a workhouse official that he could get seventeen free meals a day. The class finds some amusement in combinations for the annoyance of obnoxious unions and relieving officers. In one union, an organised gang has been turning up in the middle of the night, after the public-houses are closed, and knocking up the relieving officer. In kindness to the men themselves, as well as for reasons of public policy (for the example is contagious), guardians should be given larger powers of detention. The life of the casual would then have less temptation, and the chances of reformation and escape would not be so hopeless. The class is a perfectly artificial one, and would disappear if our law did not offer such facilities for its growth and maintenance.

Next, with regard to the sick and afflicted poor. Previous to Mr. Gathorne Hardy's Act of 1867, sick, lunatic and imbecile paupers were in most cases retained in the same buildings as the other paupers. In 1866 there were in all the London workhouses only 111 nurses, and only three trained night nurses; the rest of the service was performed by the able-bodied paupers. A doctor in private practice was paid a salary to look after the patients in the workhouse, and to supply drugs and medicine. A few lunatics were sent to the county asylums, and some patients suffering from infectious disorders obtained admission into the London Fever and Small-Pox Hospitals. Since the passing of Hardy's

Act, there are now at least 11,000 beds in separate infirmaries, many of them in every respect equal to hospitals. There are more than 1,000 trained nurses. In every infirmary there is a resident medical superintendent and an assistant, who give all their time to the inmates of the wards. The Metropolitan Asylums Board has under its charge hospitals at Hampstead, Homerton, Fulham, Deptford and Stockwell. Ambulance stations are in telephonic communication with the head office, and when a case of fever or small-pox is reported, an ambulance with a nurse and assistant is shortly at the door of the patient. There is also a service of ambulance steamers, to convey patients to two hospital ships at Purfleet. These have accommodation for about 300. At Darenth there is a hospital camp, used principally as a place of convalescence. Under the same Board there are lunatic asylums at Leavesden, Caterham and Darenth, with accommodation for about 6,000. At Darenth there is a separate establishment for imbecile children, where no effort is spared to give education and training to those who are at all able to profit by it. The Board further has a training ship, the 'Exmouth,' to which boys who wish to go to sea are sent from the metropolitan pauper schools. These boys, as a rule, go into the Navy or mercantile marine. As might have been expected, the great advantages offered in these various establishments have tended largely to increase the number of paupers.

In addition to the infirmary, there is in every union one or more poor law dispensaries. Applicants unable to provide medical treatment for themselves can apply for a doctor's order from the relieving officer. This entitles them to be treated at the dispensary, or if they are unable to go there at their own homes, and to receive such medicines as the doctor may order. In strictly administered unions, doctor's orders are given on loan, and the amount charged can be recovered from the patients when they are able to pay.

Nor has the important question of education failed to share in the increased advantages which the legislature has put at the disposal of the pauper classes of the country.

In 1867, the Metropolitan Common Poor Fund was established. On this fund is thrown the entire maintenance of children in separate schools; and as a further inducement to guardians to send all children under their charge away from the pauper influences of the workhouse, the allowance of 5*d.* per head from the common fund, payable to unions in respect of each indoor pauper, cannot be claimed for children. If children are retained in the workhouse, their maintenance falls entirely on the local rate.

Separate schools, in pursuance of this policy,

have been built in the suburbs of London, at Leavesden, Plashet, Mitcham, Norwood, Southall, Harold Court, Edmonton, Sutton, Anerley, Ashford, and Banstead. The elder children devote about half the day to industrial training. Sewing, cooking, and laundry work are taught to the girls; and the boys are instructed in farm work, carpentry, tailoring, shoemaking, baking, &c. Attached to many of the schools are drill-masters, band-masters, and teachers of swimming. The boys appear to do well in after-life. Many of them go into the naval and military bands. There is an excellent charity which provides Homes for Working Boys in London. This association is of the greatest service to guardians in looking after workhouse boys in their first start in life. The 16th Annual Report of the Local Government Board, 1886-87, gives the following particulars as to the trades adopted by boys educated in the schools belonging to the Metropolitan Unions:—

Bakers	66
Naval and military bands	153
Domestic service	43
Hairdressers	21
Homes, training or working	86
Navy	78
Mercantile marine	52
Shoemakers	55
Tailors	45
Other employments	109
Total	708

Many of these boys are born in the unskilled labour class, their passage through the district schools enables them to start in life with better prospects than many children in the rank of life from which they are drawn. Incidentally we heard the other day of two boys from these schools, who had attained the honourable position of regimental band-masters.

Of 460 girls, 456 went into domestic service. With regard to the girls, it is admitted that school life is not so advantageous. This appears to be a view taken in all ranks of life. The matter, however, is mainly one of administration. The management of some schools leaves little to be desired. An interesting experiment is being made by the Whitechapel Board of Guardians, which is worth quoting, in order to show that all boards of guardians are not so callous and indifferent to the interests of the children under their care as some critics would have us believe. A certain number of girls each year pass through a small domestic establishment, in which they are taught to do their own marketing and house-keeping. They go out and buy their own provisions, and learn, under the careful supervision of a matron, such knowledge of the value of money and of the world as a working-class housekeeper should have.

The following table is taken from the report,

1887, of the Metropolitan Association for Befriending Young Servants. One branch of the work of this most useful charity has for its object the care of girls who leave the pauper schools for domestic service. It is a summary of periodical reports sent to various boards of guardians.

	1887	1886
[1] Very good	916	821
[2] Fairly good	782	744
[3] Unsatisfactory	219	205
[4] Bad	48	54
In training homes	57	31
Emigrated	20	21
Married	7	12
Dead	8	9
Unfit for service	42	38
Visits refused	17	12
Lost sight of, or not traced	68	66
Returned to relations	95	64
In service too short a time to be reported	47	35
Total	2,326	2,112 [5]

[1] Those who throughout the year have been spoken of as satisfactory in conduct and work.

[2] Those against whom no serious faults have been alleged.

[3] Those accused of serious faults—dishonesty, untruth, extreme violence of temper, &c.

[4] Those known to have lost character, or who have been in prison for theft, &c.

[5] About 250 in 1887 and 230 in 1886 were from industrial and other non-poor law schools.

It must be remembered that many of the children remain only a short time in the schools, that they are drawn from the lowest class of the population, that, when they return to the world, they are liable to be led astray by disreputable relations; also that many of the children, permanently in the charge of the guardians, and from whom the most satisfactory results are expected, are boarded out, and therefore not included in this return. Considering all this, the result cannot be said to be unsatisfactory.

The legislature is not, however, blind to the difficulty of dealing satisfactorily with children of this class in masses. For this reason the cottage home principle of school has been adopted. From twenty to twenty-five children are placed in each, and the result is said to be encouraging, though more costly than the other system.

An Order of 1870 provides for the boarding out of deserted and orphan children. Under this arrangement children can be boarded out in the country with foster parents, under the supervision of a voluntary local committee of ladies and gentlemen. The plan has much to recommend it, as the pauper children are thus more readily merged into the general population. There appear to be numbers of poor people in some parts of the country willing to receive pauper children, but this by no means is a proof that they are always competent and worthy of the trust. The report of Miss Mason, the Government Inspector, is not a record of unchequered success. The system is proceeding quite as fast as is wise or practicable. In the opinion of competent authorities, an ill-managed system of boarding out is open to far more abuses than even an ill-managed school. Properly managed, both are useful and indispensable.

In 1862, the Local Government Board was empowered to certify non-pauper schools for the reception of pauper children, and guardians have power to pay for their maintenance there out of the rates. Under this provision Roman Catholic and Jewish schools receive the children of their own communion. Some of these schools are models of good administration.

Guardians have also power to provide special education for deaf, blind, and afflicted children. They have also authority to pay for the emigration of orphan or deserted children to the colonies.

Such, then, in outline is the provision made by law for the relief of the poor of London. Many interwoven motives have prompted a system which has grown up bit by bit since the days of Elizabeth. We might attempt to summarise, and say that in dealing with misfortunes, such as lunacy and imbecility, the law aims at relief, without any ulterior motive. The safety of society obliges it to deal effectively with cases of infectious disorder. Further, with regard to children the law appears to aim at the dispauperisation of the future generation. We seem frankly to have abandoned the view urged by the late Mr. Fawcett, the last of the economists. He was of opinion that the superior advantages given by the State to pauper children encouraged the poor to think too lightly of the responsibility of parentage. Rightly or wrongly, it is held by the majority that the object in view, dispauperisation, can be best attained in effectively, by use of the machinery of the State, returning pauper children to the ranks of economic society. It is assumed tacitly that this plan is more efficacious than any attempt to increase the sense of parental responsibility, and to rely on it as a check on the production of unprovided for children. Undoubtedly pauper children often start in life with distinctly better prospects than the children of the class from which they are drawn. The subject presents a dilemma which it is difficult to resolve.

So far the law may be said to aim at alleviation and cure, and not to concern itself with prevention. But in the rest of its policy it clearly attaches much importance to prevention. The main hope of preventing pauperism is by quickening in the character of the poor the motives which make for independence. Too great facilities for obtaining relief act as a narcotic on these salutary instincts. The law therefore attaches to relief unacceptable conditions. It assumes an individualistic basis of society. Each member of society must find an economic maintenance for himself and those dependent on him. It is easier for him to do so than for the State to do it for him. Maintenance found by the State is uneconomic. Work exacted in return for such maintenance is not economic wage-work. It is required only for purposes of discipline, or as a test of destitution. The policy of the law is clear, but in handing over its administration to boards of guardians great latitude of practice has been permitted. The Poor Law Commissioners laid it down (and the truth of the assertion is obvious) that all relief given to paupers at their own homes is inconsistent with the principle that the condition of the pauper, even in appearance, should be less eligible than that of the independent labourer of the lowest class. The exceptions, permitted by subsequent orders of the commissioners, have enabled guardians entirely to evade the rule laid down in this maxim.

The law, while being alleviative of destitution, is intended to be preventive of pauperism or dependence by enforcing motives of prudence and thrift. To alleviate suffering is not to cure pauperism. To pension an old man or woman, or to cure a sick person at the public charges, advances us no step nearer that much hoped for condition of things when the working classes will be able to do this for themselves. This is the goal, of which all who have regard for the dignity of human life refuse to despair. Let us see how far the administration of the law in the hands of guardians contributes to this result. Great issues, closely affecting the habits and character of the poor, turn on the discretion with which guardians use their power. We can only find space to say a few words on one part of the subject, namely, on the administration of out-door relief. The guardians have power to relieve the sick, the aged, and widows in this way.

We consider first the case of the sick. As a matter of fact, some portion of the working classes of this country succeed, by means of clubs and provident dispensaries, in insuring themselves against the not unusual misfortune of sickness and accident. Others neglect to make this provision, some perhaps cannot. There are admittedly large possibilities within the reach of the labouring poor. It appears to be incontestable that provident medical clubs and dispensaries flourish most where the poor law is strictly administered. In country unions of this character, even although wages are only ten shillings to fifteen shillings a week, a strong and healthy growth of solvent clubs and friendly societies has sprung up. If the gratuitous services of the parish doctor are called for, guardians closely examine into the matter, and if the patient is able, he is called on to pay as soon as he recovers from his illness. This careful administration prevents the improvident from taking advantage of their more careful neighbours, and fosters habits of prudence and self-respect in this and all other relations of life. On the other hand, in London and in most country unions the principle of economic independence has been apparently abandoned. Free hospitals and free dispensaries abound, and as a rule guardians exercise but little supervision over the medical relief which their officers give. In Manchester, where a strict administration prevails, there are a number of successful provident dispensaries, affiliated on terms of honourable self-support to the great hospitals of the town. Miss Octavia Hill, in her evidence before the Lords Committee, stated that she, acting with some of her friends among the working class, had found it impossible to start successfully a provident dispensary in Marylebone, while in Hampstead, where there is no large system of free hospitals, no such difficulty was experienced. It seems, therefore, best for guardians to offer the infirmary in sick cases, a more adequate but less eligible form of relief than an allowance given at the sick person's home. Apart from the question of principle, removal to the infirmary is in many cases best for the patients. If they have not had prudence to insure themselves against the time of sickness, they are probably persons of a careless life, and their homes are not sufficiently comfortable to make them the proper abode of sickness. Further, there is no guarantee that at home the nourishment supplied by the rates will be given to the patient. Mr. Jones, the relieving officer in

Stepney, in his evidence before the Lords, gives a horrible picture of the way in which disreputable relations deprive a sick person of delicacies and stimulants supplied by the order of the doctor.

The same line of argument applies to the maintenance provided by the rates for old age. Unless we abandon altogether the hope that the working classes can ever make provision for old age, the utmost circumspection must be exercised by guardians. Some members of the working class purchase Post-Office annuities, or subscribe to superannuation funds in their clubs, or (if a large family has prevented them from saving) they have the advantage of the assistance of their children. It is obviously unfair for the rates to give to an unthrifty man the provision which a thrifty man with only the same opportunities has secured for himself. Nor is the influence of out-door relief without injurious effects on the best instincts of family life. Cardinal Manning has strangely mistaken the effects of the system. He has complained that the restriction of out-door relief has tended to destroy family ties. One of the most painful experiences to those who visit among the London poor, is the frequent indifference of children to the fate of their aged parents. The Irish poor should be excepted from this indictment, for they have not been long enough under the baneful influence of the English poor law. It is made the interest of sons to keep out of the way, to allow their parents to increase their income from the relief office pay-table. Such a course gives a parent a little trouble, but otherwise the relief is given under fairly eligible conditions. Naturally (we do not blame them, but the state of the law), many sons will allow their parents to receive out-door relief, but they will come forward and support them rather than allow them to go into the house. Those who know the London poor must often have heard an old man or woman say, when asked as to the whereabouts of a son, that they have not heard of him for years, though often he lives in the same town. The best authorities deliberately maintain that this evil is fostered by the present system of out-door relief.

Next, with regard to widows; it frequently happens that a young widow is left with a larger family than she is able by her own earnings to support. She must seek assistance from her friends and relations, and failing them (and they probably will fail if out relief can be obtained) she must apply to the parish. The guardians can give her out relief, or offer to take some of her children to the district schools. She naturally wishes to keep all her children about her, and this she cannot do unless she gets out-door relief. There appears to be a strong case for granting it, but a closer examination of the results which follow a wholesale adoption of this course will cause us to modify our opinion. The separation of parent and child appears on careful consideration to be the lesser of two evils. If it be urged that undue suffering is involved in this course, it must be remembered that poverty is always an evil, and that hardship cannot altogether be avoided in whatever way relief is given. It may also be stated that widows, while objecting to send their children to rate-supported pauper schools, as a rule gladly welcome an offer of maintenance in an orphanage or charity school. It would appear, therefore, that their reluctance to accept this form of relief arises more from a feeling of pride than from maternal solicitude. Again, it has been pointed out by Mr. H. Longley in his report on the administration of out-door relief in London,[1] that it is not altogether impossible for a workman to make some provision for his widow. A small sum saved and the proceeds of a life-insurance policy will often be sufficient to carry the family on till the elder children are able to earn. If the widows of men who neglect this precaution are put in the same position as those whose husbands have spared and saved, it is obvious that a serious discouragement is given to working-class independence.

Further, a woman left in this position is obliged to work for her living, for the parish allowance is

[1] *Third Annual Report*, Local Government Board, 1873–1874.

of the scantiest measure, and it is perfectly impossible for her to look after a large number of young children. The consequence too often is that, when a woman attempts to maintain a large family by the help of out-door relief, she is obliged to neglect either her work or her children, and not unfrequently her health and strength break down under the strain. Guardians, therefore, in the best administered unions make it a rule that widows may be expected to maintain and look after one or two children. If they have a larger family and cannot maintain it, an offer is made to take some of the children into the district school.

Generally the system of out-door relief encourages speculative application to the rates. Discrimination on the part of guardians, both as to character and earnings, amid a population which too often regards the poor law officer and the rates as fair objects for deception, is impossible. Ingenuity and industry are misapplied in attempting to get an increase of allowances. The whole atmosphere of the family and of the neighbourhood becomes tainted with the dull dependent spirit of pauperism. Early marriages and large families appear rather an advantage than otherwise, and the doctrine is widely advertised, that the State can or will be responsible for the maintenance of all comers into this over-stocked world. Out-door relief, further, has a tendency to lower wages. For a woman who gets a few shillings a week from the parish can undersell the labour of those who are entirely dependent on their wages, or of those who, having husbands or fathers to support them, are not obliged to accept starvation wages, but are able to compete 'intelligently' with their employers.

With regard to the whole question of out-door relief, it may further be urged that as a practical measure it is not satisfactory. Adequate out-door relief is rarely given ; not a few cases of starvation have occurred in which the sufferers were in receipt of out-door relief. In 1876, to take at random one year, fourteen per cent. of the deaths from starvation of adults in London were those of persons in receipt of out-door relief. Guardians always, and often rightly, assume that applicants for relief have not fully disclosed their resources. It is also utterly fallacious to argue that out-door relief is a saving to the rates. Ten persons will apply for and receive out-door relief for every one that will accept relief in the house. A pauper costs 10*s.* in the house, but will get on with 4*s.* outside the house, but if ten persons receive 4*s.* to every one who receives 10*s.* the advantage very soon disappears. The truth of this has been proved over and over again. Yet it is surprising to learn that this fallacious argument was trotted out with great solemnity before the Lords Committee. The cost is, however, a matter of minor importance, though it might be urged that even that most despicable beast of burden, the ratepayer, has some claim to consideration.

CHAPTER XII

THE POOR LAW, CONTINUED

THESE arguments appear, perhaps, to be too theoretic, and it may be worth while to give a few figures which will beyond all doubt establish the fact that the poor rate and the number of paupers may be enormously decreased by a strict administration of the law. Evidence can also be produced to show that the hardship involved cannot be weighed against the many advantages which the plan possesses.

For some fifteen years a strict administration of the law has been pursued in three of the poorest unions in London—Whitechapel, Stepney, and St. George's in the East.

The following table, which has been published by Mr. Vallance, the clerk of the Whitechapel Union, shows the course of administration from 1870 to 1888. The figures taken are those for the sixth week of the quarter ending Lady Day.

Table showing Diminution of Pauperism in Whitechapel Union.

	In-door Paupers relieved	Out-door Paupers relieved	Total No of Paupers relieved, exclusive of Lunatics in Asylums	Ratio per cent.		Cost of Out-door Relief per week
				In-door	Out-door	£ s. d.
1870	1,419	5,339	6,758[1]	21	79	168 17 4
1871	1,219	2,568	3,787	32	68	120 14 3
1872	1,000	1,568	2,568	39	61	75 18 7
1873	1,163	845	2,008	58	42	50 4 5
1874	1,154	609	1,763	65	35	36 11 1
1875	1,170	346	1,516	77	23	22 9 0
1876	1,268	186	1,454	88	12	16 19 7
1877	1,203	122	1,325	91	9	12 2 9
1878	1,221	141[3]	1,362	90	10	11 0 6
1879	1,431[2]	143[3]	1,574	91	9	9 15 3
1880	1,464[2]	128[3]	1,592	92	8	9 7 7
1881	1,582[2]	121[3]	1,703	93	7	8 17 4
1882	1,478[2]	105[3]	1,583	93	7	7 6 11
1883	1,482[2]	91[3]	1,573	94	6	4 8 10
1884	1,418[2]	77[3]	1,495	95	5	4 2 9
1885	1,370[2]	74[3]	1,444	95	5	4 8 1
1886	1,305[2]	70[3]	1,375	95	5	3 3 5
1887	1,247[2]	61[3]	1,308	95	5	2 7 11
1888	1,356[2]	63[3]	1,419	95	5	2 10 11

[1] The figures for 1870 may be regarded as exceptional to the extent of about 2,000 paupers, there being at that period a severe temporary pressure upon the administration; but it is nevertheless interesting to note that the experience of the winter of 1869–70 induced the guardians to voluntarily suspend the Out-door Relief Regulation Order early in the following year, and to apply strictly the principle of the Out-door Relief Prohibitory Order.

[2] Including 165 imbeciles at Asylums in 1879, 162 in 1880, 159 in 1881, 152 in 1882, 140 in 1883, 135 in 1884, 130 in 1885, 126 in 1886, 127 in 1887, and 127 in 1888, not classified as 'In-door Paupers' in previous years.

[3] These figures include 30 boarded-out children in 1878, 36 in 1879, 42 in 1880, 52 in 1881, 55 in 1882, 60 in 1883, 49 in 1884, 49 in 1885, 54 in 1886, 48 in 1887, and 41 in 1888.

The next table shows the state of things at a more normal period of the year, when the winter pressure had passed, and gives also the total cost of out-door relief for each year.

	Paupers Relieved 3rd Week of April			Cost of Out Relief in Money and Kind, years ending Lady-Day
	In-door (1)	Out-door (2)	Total (3)	(4)
				£
1869	1,232	2,903	4,135	7,458
1870	1,202	2,790	3,992	6,685
1871	942	2,163	3,105	6,073
1872	952	1,261	2,213	4,730
1873	1,062	761	1,823	2,654
1874	1,101	506	1,607	2,114
1875	1,149	274	1,423	1,406
1876	1,166	156	1,322	916
1877	1,158	153	1,311	873
1878	1,138	124	1,262	731
1879	1,316	113	1,429	592
1880	1,256	104	1,360	546
1881	1,382	105	1,487	528
1882	1,352	90	1,442	584
1883	1,402	92	1,494	521
1884	1,362	73	1,435	463
1885	1,227	70	1,297	309
1886	1,148	71	1,219	167
1887	1,151	66	1,217	131
1888	1,264	48	1,312	117

NOTE.—It is to be observed that in 1869 and 1870 the imbecile paupers were maintained in the workhouse and were enumerated in Col. 1. In 1871 those paupers had been transferred to Imbecile Asylums and had ceased to be so enumerated until 1879 when they were required to be again included in the return of in-door paupers. This will explain the sudden diminution in in-door paupers in 1871 and the sudden rise in 1879. It will thus be seen that the numbers of paupers relieved in 1869 and 1888 respectively are fairly comparable; excepting that considerable allowance must be made from the numbers of in-door paupers in the later years for the increase which has taken place in the number of sick poor relieved, occasioned by the improved provision for that class of poor in separate infirmaries.

It appears from the above that there is an annual saving of some 6,000*l.*, and a total diminution of some 2,800 paupers, without any appreciable difference in the number of the in-door paupers.

After the strict system had been in operation for some time the Whitechapel board ordered a careful enquiry to be made as to the result of their action. Dr. Billing, now Bishop of Bedford, and the Rev. S. A. Barnett were for many years members of the Whitechapel board, and no one who knows Mr. Vallance will accuse him or his board of making statements which they cannot substantiate.

The following is the result of the enquiry :—

RETURN OF THE WHITECHAPEL UNION.

Analysis of Cases in which Out-relief to able-bodied widows or deserted wives has been discontinued by the Guardians, from Lady Day, 1873, *to Lady Day*, 1875.

	Cases	Individs.	Cases	Individs.
Total number of cases other than temporary cases of sickness in which out-relief has been discontinued			167	600
Doing as well or better as when in receipt of out-relief, without further assistance			77	270
Getting an independent living, having had assistance :—				
By admission of children to industrial schools (18 children have been admitted)	11	49		
By assistance received from children	7	11		
By change of circumstances . .	4	14		
By return of neglecting husbands .	4	18		
Married	4	18		
By assistance through Charity Organisation Society	7	28		
By assistance through Jewish Board .	5	26		
By employment in Workhouse . .	8	38		
By assistance from Blind Society .	2	2		
	—	—	52	204

			Cases	Individs.
Present whereabouts not known			17	76
Admitted to Workhouse			10	11
Dead			2	2
Removed under order of removal			1	4
Not supposed to be doing well, caused by—	Cases	Individs.		
Drunken habits	2	11		
By refusal to send children to District School	4	16		
By careless and dirty habits	1	2		
'Not doing as well as she might'	1	4	8	33
			167	600

The above refers to a limited class, but it displays, to use a geological term, a section of the result of the Whitechapel administration.

The reduction of out-door pauperism in Whitechapel was somewhat gradual, as the above tables will show. In the neighbouring union of St. George in the East the change was made more suddenly. The following particulars are taken from a pamphlet by Mr. A. G. Crowder, a guardian of that union, who took a leading part in the change that was then made:—

On January 1, 1875, the number of paupers in St. George's in the East (population about 47,000, and the district as poor as any in London) was 3,047. Of these 1,248 were in receipt of in-door relief and 1,799 of out-door relief. The guardians *suddenly* set to work to revise their out-door relief list, with the result that on Jan. 1, 1876, the numbers were—in-door 1,258, out-door 548, total 1,806.

These figures are very remarkable. In one year two-thirds of the out-door relief was stopped, with the addition of only ten paupers to the in-door list. But the matter becomes intelligible when Mr. Crowder tells us that the cost of the out-door relief given per week to each pauper averaged less than one shilling. That is to say, $1\frac{5}{7}d.$ per day. The average allowance in out-door relief unions is not very different at the present time.

In Fulham	in 1887 it was under		$2\frac{2}{7}d.$	per day
In Bethnal Green	,,	,,	$2\frac{1}{7}d.$	,,
In Islington	,,	,,	$2\frac{2}{7}d.$	,,
All London	,,	,,	$3\frac{3}{28}d.$	,,

The above, it is understood, includes the cost of funerals, so that the allowance to the living is even less.

Mr. Crowder goes on to state the steps which he took to satisfy himself that the reform did not involve undue hardship on the poor.

I attended (he says) regularly at the relief meetings of the board, and I carefully entered in a note-book the seemingly hard cases. I waited a week or two, and then personally visited the homes of these people. What I saw satisfied me that the hardship was not great. . . . In many instances the guardians had been imposed upon, and the people were better off than had been supposed; in others relations, friends, or the charitable had come forward, especially in the case of widows with children, and sick cases; in others energy had been aroused and better work maintained; very few had migrated into laxer districts, and those who had did not obtain relief, as they would not have been eligible under a year's residence, and comparatively few, about one-third, had accepted the test offer of the Workhouse Pauper School.

This personal testimony bears out in every particular the statistical information supplied by the Whitechapel board. With regard to the alleged fact that paupers migrate from the strict to the laxer districts, Mr. Vallance has elsewhere stated that his union transfers more paupers as chargeable to other unions than it receives. A year's residence is necessary to qualify for relief in any union, and unfortunately the pauper class does not look forward one year even for the purpose of obtaining out-door relief.

The foregoing statements, however, deal mainly with the case of widows with children. It is necessary to say something with regard to the aged and infirm poor. Mr. Vallance states with regard to his union :—

> The aged and infirm were only relieved out of doors when there was evidence of thrift, and when the guardians were satisfied that there were no children or relatives legally or morally liable to support them and able to do so ; but even this class became non-existent by the establishment of the Tower Hamlets Pension Fund, with the benevolent object of saving the really deserving poor from the poor law.

Mr. Vallance maintains, and his view is justified by the course of events in these three unions, that when the guardians restrict themselves to their proper function of relieving destitution, the charitable public will come forward and deal with the exceptional cases.

Destitution can only be discovered by offering to an applicant, whose income it is impossible to discover with certainty, a maintenance which is perfectly adequate, but which he will not exchange for his own mode of living unless he is absolutely obliged. These conditions can only be fulfilled, say the Poor Law Commissioners, by an offer of maintenance in a well regulated workhouse.

The method of the Stepney board is of value as a practical illustration of how such reforms can be carried out. The guardians caused strict investigation to be made as to the character and antecedents of the recipients of out-door relief. This caused a certain diminution in the list. The relieving officers were next instructed to see that each old or infirm pauper had an income of at least 1*s.* a day from all sources. Guardians often found themselves obliged to supply 5*s.*, 6*s.*, or even 7*s.* per week to make up this sum. They naturally were more careful than when they were doling out shillings and half-crowns. As a result the list diminished to such modest limits that the charities of the district were able to undertake the care of exceptional cases, and the guardians were able to act on a uniform rule.

The table opposite shows the result of the administration of the law in Stepney.

STEPNEY UNION.

A Return of the Numbers of Inmates Relieved in the Poplar and Stepney Sick Asylum, the Bromley and Poplar Workhouses, and the several Schools in connection with the above Union, as well as the numbers who received Out-door Relief during the several Half-years ending as below; together with the cost of In-door Maintenance and the amount paid in Out-door Relief during the same periods, also the number of Men, Women and Children who received Out-door Medical Attendance only.

Half-year ending Lady-day	In-door Poor Classification				The Half-yearly Cost of In-door Maintenance	Out-door Poor Classification				The Half-yearly cost of Out-door relief	In addition, the following received Out-door Medical Attendance only			
	Men	Women	Childrn.	Total	£	Men	Women	Childrn.	Total	£	Men	Women	Childrn.	Total
1869	509	526	673	1,708	6,344	1,301	2,354	3,947	7,602	6,153	391	1,011	1,018	2,420
1870	549	527	618	1,694	6,084	1,161	1,982	3,206	6,349	5,934	372	811	1,047	2,230
1871	455	448	536	1,439	4,876	754	1,521	2,140	4,415	5,401	299	640	672	1,611
1875	556	505	520	1,581	4,543	101	296	144	541	1,200	373	294	155	822
1879	648	501	514	1,663	4,894	53	157	53	263	686	335	356	100	791
1883	661	509	535	1,705	5,425	34	77	24	135	362	383	376	165	924
1886	773	524	529	1,826	[1] 5,809	26	53	17	96	250	413	487	208	1,113
1887	655	523	492	1,670	[1] 5,389	28	49	18	95	218	379	477	199	1,055

Memoranda.—During the 1st week, Midsummer, 1869, the Out-door Weekly Relief amounted to £219 0 0
" " " 1883 " " " 11 13 4
" 5th " 1884 " " " 10 10 6
" 6th " Christmas, 1887 " " " 7 7 0

The total expenditure in 1869 for the half-year was £12,498. For the same period of 1887, it was only £5,607, showing a saving £6,891 for the half-year. Stepney is a district inhabited largely by the working class, and this saving at the rate of nearly £14,000 per annum is a contribution by the guardians towards lowering the rents of working class dwellings.

[1] These include the cost of maintenance of patients in Asylums (about £650), which theretofore had not been included.

Wherever a strict system has been tried, the same results have been attained. To see the full effect, however, of the system it is necessary to go to the country. In London the areas of administration are comparatively small, and the population is fluctuating. The sound system of administration, which has reduced the rate of pauperism in Whitechapel to 16 per 1,000 has to contend with the profligate administration of the City of London Union. The City of London is probably more largely endowed with charities than any other place in the world, and one might have thought that poor law relief would be almost unnecessary. What, however, is the fact? The lax administration has made paupers of 62 persons in every 1,000, or nearly four times the rate of the poor union of Whitechapel. This pauper Alsatia on the borders of Whitechapel cannot fail to counteract the dispauperising influence of the better system.

Going, therefore, to the country to a union of 62,977 acres, with a stationary agricultural population, it will be possible to see the system tried under fairer conditions. We select the union of Bradfield, Berks. The statistical result of 17 years' wise administration is as follows :—

BRADFIELD UNION.

Comparative Statement of Pauperism on Jan. 1, 1871, *to* 1888, *inclusive. Population*, 1871, 15,853; 1881, 17,972; *acreage*, 62,977.

	Paupers on Jan. 1		Total	Proportion to population 1 in	Rate in the pound
	In-door	Out-door			
					d.
1871	999	259	1,258	13	$24\frac{1}{2}$
1872	835	214	1,049	15	$21\frac{1}{4}$
1873	750	200	950	16	19
1874	604	184	788	20	$18\frac{1}{2}$
1875	610	174	784	20	$13\frac{1}{2}$
1876	482	154	636	25	$12\frac{1}{4}$
1877	349	140	489	32	$10\frac{1}{2}$
1878	279	152	431	37	$10\frac{3}{4}$
1879	234	135	369	43	$9\frac{1}{2}$
1880	181	138	319	49	9
1881	202	151	353	45	9
1882	142	151	293	61	$8\frac{1}{2}$
1883	116	144	260	69	$7\frac{3}{4}$
1884	90	146	236	76	$7\frac{3}{4}$
1885	71	136	207	87	$6\frac{3}{4}$
1886	60	120	180	100	$6\frac{1}{2}$
1887	52	110	162	111	$6\frac{1}{2}$
1888	42	100	142	126	$5\frac{3}{4}$

In 17 years' administration under the able guidance of the chairman, Mr. Bland Garland, the number of paupers has fallen from 1,258 to 142, and the rate from 2*s*. $0\frac{1}{2}$*d*. in the pound to $5\frac{3}{4}$*d*. In 1871 1 in every 13 of the population was a pauper, in 1888 1 in every 126. What has become of the 1,116 who were paupers in 1871? The following quotation from a paper read by Mr. Bland Garland at the Central Poor Law Conference on Dec. 12, 1888, will suggest the answer:—

I may be asked (he says) what effect this has had on the condition of the people. I can reply with perfect confidence that it has much improved; that it never was before so good as now, although wages are considerably less than they were in the earlier years of the period mentioned. They have learnt in a great measure to depend on their own exertions, to provide against a rainy day, to support their aged parents, and the demands on private charity are much less than when they were recipients of the miserable pauper-dole, or were looking forward to obtaining it.

I may point for confirmation to the fact that during the last three winters, although many were out of employment, not a single able-bodied man applied for relief, if I except here and there a drunken lay-about. The widows are in every respect better off than when they received out relief as a matter of course; they then lived to a great extent on private charity, and their children were much employed in begging; if these evils have not altogether ceased, they are much lessened. I may here also refer to the fact that out of forty-eight widows who have applied for out-door relief, not one, and of 184 children, only eight, were in the workhouse on January 1.

To give you direct proof of increased thrift is a more difficult task. I cannot, of course, have access to the books of the savings banks, or those of the great collecting insurance companies; but I have obtained returns of nearly all the friendly societies that are established or have branches within the union, including even the public-house clubs (the members of which have much decreased in number), and also of the medical clubs, and they show that the membership of the friendly societies has increased 148 per cent. since 1871, and that of the doctors' clubs 152 per cent. This is satisfactory as far as it goes.

This last sentence tells what has become of the vanished pauperism of Bradfield Union. They have availed themselves of an alternative, namely the principle of insurance. There is a stern struggle for existence going on in the lower stratum of labour. Population presses to overflow into any form of existence where a living is to be got. It is a question whether men will in this state of things avail themselves of the maintenance provided by the poor law or of the security that can be honourably gained by the expedient of insurance. A strict administration of the law is necessary to bring about the latter desirable result.

Unfortunately, it is impossible to produce Government statistics on this point. Saving and insurance cannot be traced locally by unions. It is, therefore, necessary to rely on personal observation such as that contained in the quotations from Mr. Bland Garland's paper. In the summer of 1888 the author received a letter from the Rev. B. Hale Puckle, chairman of the St. Neots board of guardians, in reply to a request for information on this point. He says:—

No permanent out-relief has been granted by the St. Neots board for many years, with this result, that whereas some twenty years ago it was the exception that the applicant for relief at the board belonged to a benefit club, now the exception is that an applicant does not or has not belonged to a club. I am informed by collectors of insurance payments and managers of benefit clubs, that there is more business done in this union than in any of the surrounding unions, where out relief is more largely given. I find that our medical relief is only about 100*l.* a year, on account of the increase of medical clubs and so many receiving medical attendance from their benefit club; and also from the fact that most of our medical relief is given on loan. . . I wish I could give you more accurate and statistical information, but I can only give the result of my own observation; e.g. there is not above one man, young or old, in the parish in which I live who does not belong to a club or friendly society.

There are at the present moment over 600,000 out-door paupers in England, and at least as many more qualifying themselves to take the place of the present 600,000. If the system pursued in Bradfield was adopted all over the country, the great bulk of this population of 600,000 would be restored to the ranks of honourable independence, and we might also hope to see the in-door list gradually dwindling, as appears in the table on p. 227. The benefit to the poor would be incalculable, and the saving to the rates would go far to remove the growing grievance arising out of the incidence of local taxation.

It is of course very necessary that guardians who take this strict course of administration, should spare no pains to make the management of their workhouse as humane and exemplary as is possible. The reader should refer to the evidence given by Mr. Vallance, the clerk to the Whitechapel board, before the select committee of the House of Lords. The guardians in that union rely on dissociation and continuous work as the best agencies of reform. Almost every one can use a paintbrush, and men who have trades are made to work in order to provide things required in the workhouse. The men are employed as far as possible separately. This seclusion is welcome to the respectable, and is distasteful to the idle shirking gossip. The much decried oakum-picking and stone-breaking are no part of the system. The relief given is not wages but maintenance. No extra allowances are given, and the workman knows that he must rely on work obtained under ordinary conditions if he wishes to return to the world.

Well-to-do people, into whose calculations relief from the rates does not enter, find it difficult to understand the force of this insidious influence on the lives of the poor. It may be possible to bring it home to them by a parable. It is obvious that, if a man has a journey to make and is told that the railway company will provide him with lunch, he will not trouble himself to take a sandwich in his pocket. It is precisely the same with the journey through life; if a man is told that the rates will give him an allowance in sickness, a pension in old age, employment in a labour yard when work is slack, and that his wife will be provided for when he is dead, it clearly becomes unnecessary for him to do any of these things for himself.

Before considering the reforms which are practicable, we must finish our survey of the whole subject. It becomes therefore necessary to consider a matter which has of late been much before the public, namely, the question of the 'Unemployed.' The unemployed in London have been mainly unskilled labourers, young men, mere lads who have not yet got a suitable job, or old men past their work and who have made no provision for their old age, men who always have lived on their wives and relations, men with intermittent work, or men whose trades are always slack in the winter, and the large nondescript and unfortunate class which one can only describe under the general term of loafers, with a proportion, a smaller proportion, probably, than is generally represented, of really employable workmen.

Various suggestions are made. Relief works must be started, a demand for labour will always produce labour; witness the growth of population in the north of England. Relief works mean practically an unlimited demand for unskilled labour. An unlimited supply of the 'unemployed' is not a result to be contemplated with equanimity. Nor are recommendations for the adoption of the Dutch or German system of beggar colonies very much to the point. Everywhere the pressure of human life is seeking to overflow the limits of maintenance provided by existing economic conditions. By adopting the Dutch or German system we can of course produce the Dutch or German type of pauper, but the same problem remains, and we must search for its solution in some other direction. The safety of society depends on the majority of its members finding for themselves economic conditions of survival. The State is exceeding its functions if it weights the poorer classes of society with the competition of an uneconomic or parasitic class, which it allows to go at large and to disturb the labour market of the provident poor. It should not encourage the growth of such a class by offering eligible conditions of relief. When it has to relieve members of this class, it should remove them for the time being from the market, and so prevent them from prejudicing the interest of their more provident neighbours. These two conditions can only be fulfilled by an offer of maintenance within the walls of a well regulated workhouse.

Mr. Charles Booth, in his valuable paper on the Condition and Occupations of the People of East London and Hackney, read before the Statistical Society on May 15, 1888, has summed up the problem in the following words:—

To the rich the 'very poor' are a sentimental interest; to the 'poor' they are a crushing load. The poverty of the poor is mainly the result of the competition of the very poor. The entire removal of this class out of the daily struggle for existence I believe to be the only solution of the problem of poverty. Is this solution beyond our reach? If it is true, as we are taught, and as I believe, that the standard of life is rising, and that the proportion of the population in very poor circumstances never has been less, and is steadily decreasing, it follows, as I think, that some day the individualist community on which we build our faith will find itself obliged, for its own sake, to take charge of the lives of those who, from whatever cause, are incapable of independent existence up to the required standard, and will be fully able to do so. Has this time come yet? [1]

It is easier to ask than to answer the question.

One very obvious cause of the dearth of demand for unskilled labour is to be found in the increasing

[1] The above is from the original paper read by Mr. Booth. He has since amplified the latter part of the quotation in the larger volume which he has published on the *Labour and Life of the People*. The statement of the position is admirable, and Mr. Booth's confession of faith in individualism seemed as rare as it was admirable. We should never have suspected that the ambiguous sentence at the end meant that individualistic society should embark on new socialistic experiments. This, however, is the turn which Mr. Booth's fuller treatment of the subject takes. His plea is for a never-ceasing dispersion or 'harrying' (the expression is his own) of the lapsed classes. For ourselves, we do not believe in artificial 'harrying'—it is vacillating and uncertain; we should rather be content to leave the correction of incompetence and error to the punitive force of nature, mitigated by an offer of maintenance under discipline, and coupled, in the interest of independent competitors, with enforced withdrawal from the labour market.

use of machinery. We cannot go back to the times when everything was done by manual labour. Unskilled labour is daily becoming less necessary. Even the agricultural labourer is called on to look after machinery. Man is becoming a machine-using as well as a property-owning animal. Machinery is one of the elements in which he has to learn to move. The labourer who cannot use machinery is, to use evolutionary language, becoming unfitted.

He might, however, if there was effective demand for more of the products of industry, find employment in the less skilled departments of manufacture. How is this consummation to be brought about?

An ingenious American economist, Mr. Gunton, in his work 'Wealth and Progress' (a book which has attracted less attention in this country than it deserves), has pointed out that 80 per cent. of the manufactured articles of industry are consumed by the working classes. He comes, therefore, to the pleasant conclusion that if wages were only higher there would be an increased demand throughout 80 per cent. of the trade of the world. We are all with Mr. Gunton in wishing to see wages doubled, particularly our own, but as it is not possible to bring this about at a stroke, it would be well to consider whether the spending of the wages we have is as wisely conducted as could be wished.

It is to be feared that all wages are not spent productively. The working classes of this country voluntarily pay an enormous share of the taxation of the empire. Leaving out of sight the cost of the alcoholic liquor itself, the excise and duties paid on this and on tobacco amount to the enormous sum of 45,000,000*l.* This sum goes to pay for the expense of government and the maintenance of our army and navy. If the working classes ceased to furnish the exchequer with their voluntary offering, new direct taxes would have to be devised, and the deficiency would have to be made up out of the pockets of the richer classes. These would have to give up some of their luxuries which do not as a rule give employment to much labour, but their labour-employing expenditure would not be curtailed. The money retained by the working classes and not spent in drink would be saved, and through our banking system invested in machinery which would give additional employment to some, or it would be spent in maintaining a regular, steady demand throughout all the domestic industries of the country, and want of employment would be thus reduced.

This difficulty of want of employment therefore resolves itself into a question of character and habit. By greater thrift and by greater prudence the difficulty disappears. 'Unemployedness' arises out of the uneconomic conditions into which socialistic legislation has driven people. Reform is to be sought in the removal of some of the uneconomic conditions of life, and the most obvious step, as far as our poor-law administration is concerned, is to stop out-door relief. One of the first results of this will be that wages will be better spent. When wages are well spent we shall be within reach of solving the terms of the equation which exists between the demand and supply of labour. When all wages are spent productively there will be plenty of employment for all. A wise expenditure of wages represents prudent character, and a highly developed state of the instinct of property and civilisation. This instinct, as we have shown, regulates and adjusts population to the maintenance which from time to time is supplied for it by the economic circumstances of the time.

When society has reached this happy goal we shall be within measurable distance of detecting the wasteful and unproductive expenditure of government. The impotence of the fetich of Central Government, as Mr. Spencer calls it, will be exposed. Its spawn of inspectors, its armies and navies, its incompetence, its red tape, its circumlocution, its jobbery will be reduced to a minimum, and we shall wonder how we ever came to tax ourselves to maintain a system so burdensome and oppressive.

Sir Henry Maine has conjectured that our love

of politics has some connection with our love of sport. The country gentleman of olden days took his turn at politics between the seasons of fox hunting and partridge shooting. The game of politics has now become the amusement of the democracy of the towns. It is a costly and perilous game. Few persons make any study of the history of political institutions, and every year legislation becomes more random and haphazard.

The American constitution enables the game to be carried on without serious consequence, beyond inflicting a certain burden on the rates, for as it is played in the great republic of the west the President, the State governor, and the town mayor have a right of veto which they are expected by the community to use very freely. The governor, says Mr. Bryce,[1] 'cannot shelter himself behind the will of the representatives of the people, because he is appointed to watch and check these representatives as a policeman watches a suspect.' By this ingenious contrivance, the amusement of legislators, though costly, is rendered comparatively innocuous. The English public has unfortunately no such protector from the tyranny of Parliament.

[1] *American Commonwealth*, ii. 175.

CHAPTER XIII

INSURANCE A SUBSTITUTE FOR THE POOR LAW

THE question of Poor Law administration has been treated here in some detail, for there is a possibility in this matter of some practical reform. We have therefore given a prominence in this work to considerations connected with the poor law, and can deal only in a cursory manner with other forms of State socialism, which though perhaps equally important are not yet ripe for curtailment and removal.

The advocates of the abolition of out-door relief urge that the proper alternative is to be found in the principle of insurance. Of all the modern expedients for the distribution of property and for giving to poor men the security of civilised life, insurance is perhaps the most ingenious and the most valuable. The principle of insurance has been widely applied, and it is capable of much wider extension. There is hardly any risk which is incapable of being insured. The professional classes are admirably served by commercial enterprise, and their wants are in this way adequately met.

In America life insurance is the principal form of saving. It has been less extensively used on the continent of Europe, perhaps for the reason that there is a wider distribution of landed property and because savings are invested in land rather than in insurance. In France, however, it is curious to note, the French peasant has insured his crops against damage by storm, a risk which is proverbially the most uncertain of all things. This fact is an interesting illustration of the principle which we are trying to enforce, namely, that when people are indoctrinated with the instincts of property (and the French peasant is a landed proprietor) they display extraordinary ingenuity in meeting responsibility in whatever shape it presents itself to them.

One of the most melancholy difficulties with which the working classes have to contend is that commercial enterprise seems unable to serve them in one or two of the most important interests of their lives.

Banking for the middle and upper classes is a profitable industry, and competition among bankers causes them to vie with one another in giving to their customers such facilities as they require. The savings of the working classes are now very large, yet commercial enterprise has not to any large extent entered this field of industry. The workman's principal savings bank is the Post Office. The Post Office, like all Government departments, is not a very enterprising institution. Its banking business is distinctly an excrescence. Its customers have to wait patiently in queue till the officials are ready to attend to them, and none but the most determined depositors can face the difficulties of the situation. To be really successful the working class banker ought to be something of a canvasser and collector of deposits, he ought to have his representatives conveniently stationed to receive payments on the wage day. The great success of institutions like the Prudential Insurance Company comes from the skilful way in which they adapt themselves to the needs and humours of their customers. A working man requires his opportunities for saving to be brought to his door, for the excellent reason that he is often overworked and has little leisure. The collecting insurance companies know what their customers want, and this is the secret of their success. It may be said that a canvassing style of banking would never have paid without lapsing into extravagant expenditure. It is, however, impossible to foresee how difficulties will be met till the attempt has been made. The ground is now covered by the Post Office, and private enterprise competes under great disadvantages with the Government banking monopoly.

Working class insurance is a matter of even greater importance than working class banking. Happily Government has not thought it necessary to supply a system of insurance against sickness, and the requirements of the working class have been satisfied by associations devised by themselves. Commercially speaking, insurance is a more complicated subject than banking, yet the great working class friendly societies have surmounted the difficulties and have started a system very well suited to their wants, and, what is very important as compared with the stereotyped plan of a Government department, capable of extension and alteration. The history of working class insurance has some points of resemblance to that of middle class insurance for fire, life, and marine risks. Originally all insurance was made on the mutual principle, that is to say, insurance associations were for mutual protection. Insurers combined and indemnified each other against loss. If a loss was incurred, a levy was made by the association for the benefit of the loser. Experience soon enabled the persons concerned to calculate the probability of loss and to fix a premium. The managers used the premiums for the transaction of financial business, and the mutual insurers shared in any surplus that was left after claims were paid.

A further development has taken place in modern imes, and insurance business is transacted by joint stock companies. The shareholders enter into the business as a form of commercial enterprise, and are not of necessity insurers at all. Many ot the older mutual companies, finding themselves very rich, have taken steps to secure the advantages of the position to their members, and new insurers enter on less advantageous terms. They act, and with perfect right and justice, as did the old gilds of mediæval times. Working class insurance is mainly against the risk of sickness, and for this reason the mutual system is found most convenient. It is only by means of the supervision of interested members that the danger of malingering can be provided against. The development of the friendly society has not proceeded beyond the mutual stage. It is stated that some of the successful lodges of the affiliated orders, finding that they have a substantial surplus over the estimated claims, close their books, and take no more members, and proceed to appropriate the realised surplus by giving increased benefits or by lowering the rate of contribution. At page 32 of the Quarterly Report, February 1889, of the Manchester Unity of Oddfellows, notice is given of a special resolution of the directors. A certain lodge, which had divided a surplus in 1875, now finds itself in a deficiency on valuation. The directors call on the lodge to make good the deficiency at once, and instruct their actuary to report to the board all cases of a similar description.

There is, therefore, a certain want of permanency in these mutual associations. The joint stock system, on the other hand, is conducted permanently for the sake of profit. The managers are obliged to keep a reserve sufficient to justify the confidence of insurers. Insurers have no claim on the profits of the business. Shareholders find that to use a portion of their capital as a reserve fund is a profitable employment of their money. They are under no temptation to deplete this fund. But in a mutual undertaking, such as a friendly society lodge, there is naturally and properly enough a desire, on the part of insurers, to divide and appropriate surplus funds. This militates against the solvency, and also against the permanency, of such institutions.

The objection is, however, inevitable, so long as sickness continues to be the main risk against which workmen insure. The great difficulty which a purely commercial enterprise would have to surmount is that sickness is incapable of exact definition, and fraudulent claims, according to present experience, can only be kept in check by the close supervision of interested parties. Societies which are managed from a central office, like the Hearts of Oak, very nearly approach to the efficiency and simplicity of commercial enterprise, but the actuary's report of 1888, addressed to members of this society, dwells very strongly on the necessity of stricter supervision over sick claims. The centralised system of sick insurance business, of which the Hearts of Oak is the most eminent example, has the advantage of greater publicity, more efficient management by experts, but it has to meet the very great difficulty of checking malingering. To the State club supported by a compulsory poll-tax, as suggested by Mr. Blackley, this difficulty would be absolutely insurmountable.

The local lodge system of friendly society can exercise stricter supervision over sick claims. It encourages friendly intercourse among members, and has a certain educational value. On the other hand, insurance is a very technical business, and actuarial knowledge is not very plentiful. The difficulty of a local want of technical knowledge is met by the system of supervision exercised by the central boards of the affiliated friendly societies. Without doubt these great orders do admirable work in enforcing sound views of insurance on the local lodges, and considering this difficulty of malingering, the lodge system has many obvious advantages.

While then insurance against sickness must apparently be provided by mutual societies only, it may be that with regard to life insurance commercial enterprise will undertake to supply what is wanted. This is an age of subdivision of labour. The professional man (except as a director in return for fees) does not want to manage his own insurance company. A workman's leisure is scanty enough, and it is difficult to see any reason why he should be left to struggle with the intricacies of actuarial science.

Life insurance is at present supplied to the working class by the Prudential, the Pearl, and other collecting industrial Insurance Companies. The Government has a system of its own, but as it omits to deliver its goods at the door of the purchaser the insurance department of the Post Office has been a complete failure. In 1887 the Post Office derived from insurance premiums an income of 13,492*l.* and paid 5,976*l.* in claims.[1] This business is mainly done, we are credibly informed, with its own employés. The Prudential Company undertakes to deliver, and makes a charge for delivery. Their customers are retail buyers and they undertake to sell retail. In its Industrial branch alone the Company received in 1888 3,256,346*l.* in premiums from the working class, and paid in claims 1,231,186*l.* In its Ordinary branch, which is largely used by the more intelligent workman, who is able to buy in larger quantities by quarterly payments,

[1] *Thirty-fourth Report of the Postmaster-General*, Appendix J. The Government statistics are naturally a year behind everyone else's.

its revenue in premiums was 718,848*l.* for the same year, and the claims paid amounted to 210,056*l.* The terms for this branch of the business will bear comparison with those of the ordinary company which supplies the upper and middle classes. With a fatuity which is almost incredible, well-meaning philanthropists have endeavoured to disparage the work of these societies, because forsooth they adapt themselves to the necessity of the case and collect the premiums weekly by house to house visitation.

A great engineer was wont to say that an invention which was no one's property remained useless to mankind ; but give a man an absolute property in it and tell him to make his fortune out of it, he busied himself to proclaim its merits, to adapt it to the requirements of trade and to present it in a saleable form to the public.

Insurance is an ingenious invention, but placed in the hands of the Post Office it remains barren ; but when manipulated and prepared for sale by commercial enterprise it supplies a social want and confers incalculable benefits on mankind.

It is not too much to say that the country owes a great debt of gratitude to these institutions. They have kept alive, during a very dark period of working class history, some small interest in the principle of insurance, some respect for this valuable expedient of survival amid the dangers of civilised life.

The philanthropists complain that these insurances rarely provide anything more than a funeral benefit. But, we ask, have not these very philanthropists been parties to the conspiracy which has taught men that the State will give a pension to their wives and children when they die? By a miracle the poor man's abhorrence of a pauper funeral has survived the machinations of the philanthropist. On this not too hardy instinct of independence the commercial companies have had to work. They employ a vast army of collectors whose interest and whose business it is to urge their customers to subscribe for life insurance and not for a mere funeral benefit. The enormous and unprecedented success of a company like the Prudential is evidence that, if the State will only withdraw its blighting influence, ordinary commercial agencies are providing the working classes with a species of property which they are willing to buy and which will protect them and theirs in a manner conformable to the laws of civilised life. The State has deprived poor men of all chance of saving by buying land; it has for long prevented them from seeing the advantage of insurance; surely the time has come when our rulers should take a more statesmanlike attitude in this matter.

The notion has been put about in this and in many other departments of life that everyone who deals with the working class should do so on elee mosynary terms. The better class of financier and builder does not care therefore to incur the risk and obloquy of catering for the working class. This very fact enables capital to demand a higher rate of interest when it is applied to the service of poor men, and this socialistic, philanthropic fallacy enormously increases what has been called the expensiveness of poverty.

To resume, insurance against sickness is supplied by Friendly Societies of genuine working class origin. The system may be capable of extension and improvement, but in most respects it is altogether admirable. Commercial enterprise has already provided and is prepared to increase opportunity for life insurance. As against these two honourable expedients for the preservation of independence, the State offers a rival system of degradation by means of out-door relief. We urge that the time has now come for some reform.

To effect this we have to appeal to the electorate. The electorate is very largely the working class, and this subject of the poor law is one to which the leaders of the working class have as yet paid very little attention. During the sittings of the select committee of the House of Lords in the summer of 1888, it was thought desirable to ascertain the views of the working class on the subject. Through Lord Spencer the committee communicated with certain of the working class representatives in the House of Commons. Their reply seems to have been (and no doubt truly) that they could not name any one of their class who had made a special study of this subject.

This is a matter much to be regretted. Lord Balfour of Burleigh, who took an active part in the proceedings of the committee, is reported to have said at the annual meeting of the Charity Organisation Society in the spring of 1889, that—

> The committee could not ascertain that the question into which we were appointed to inquire had even been discussed, either by the trades-unions or any other body representative of the working classes. That man would deserve well of his country who could discover the means of enlisting intelligent artisans and working men in the administration of the poor law.

It is impossible to exaggerate the importance of this recommendation. Workmen naturally take the view that appears at first sight generous and liberal, and have very little regard for their own interest in the matter.

As a matter of fact it affects them very closely. The workman who is developed by undue facility of poor law relief is a curse to all the best interests of his class. He is always badly off, and is a prey to every grasping employer whom he meets, and so is a cause of low wages. He does not assist the trade-union, on the contrary, his action is inimical to such combinations. He marries young and imprudently and has a large family, and so increases the competition for employment. He subscribes to no friendly society. Insurance depends on averages, and his abstention from the club causes the provident workman to pay a higher rate for his insurance. He brings up his children in the same way, and the circle of pauperism and of unintelligent competition grows wider. His expenditure of wages is foolish, it gives no employment to labour ; as likely as not it goes to support the drink monopoly and to swell the profits of the publican. Society then, growing contrite over his drunken habits, will probably have to pay an enormous compensation to the publican whose property it confiscates. Needless to say a portion of this compensation will come out of the pocket of the industrious workman. Every act of this man tends to lower not only his own status but also that of his fellows.

Finally, he becomes chargeable to the poor law, and the rate on which he is supported is added to the rent which the industrious workman has to pay for his house. Thus the difficulty of housing the town artisan is aggravated.

Surely it is not necessary to be too sentimental in dealing with this man and his dependents. Even if we wish to be generous, it is wiser to deal strictly with him, if possible to reform him by the discipline of bitter experience; anything rather than abandon him to the degradation which the present system most certainly provides for him.

It is a curious circumstance, that not a single modern writer of any repute who has dealt with this subject has a word to say in favour of out-door relief. Yet the manufactory of pauperism goes on, and no attention is paid to the teaching of precept and experience. Unions sometimes have a period of sound administration, and then lapse back again into the slough.

It is notorious that the reform of the poor law in 1834 proceeded on lines which had been proved successful by experiments made at Southwell and Bingham. It appears from present statistics that these two unions have lapsed into lax administration.[1]

The official returns show that on July 1, 1887, there were in

	In-door	Out-door	Total
Southwell	79	514	593
Bingham	65	310	375

This great preponderance of out-door over in-door relief is conclusive evidence that the recommendations of the Poor Law Commissioners are not now followed in these unions as they were at the earlier period. This is surely a curious comment on our present system.

Again, as already pointed out, the very widest differences in administration prevail in neighbour-

[1] Sir G. Nicholls, *History of Poor Law*, vol. ii. p. 241.

ing unions. It is manifestly unjust that the guardians of the City of London should be empowered by law to take money from the ratepayers in order to tempt 62 per 1,000 of the population to become paupers, while in the adjacent union of Whitechapel, a much poorer district, a wiser administration of the law has reduced the dependent population to 16 per 1,000. It is absolutely necessary that this power of guardians to burden the solvent population with the maintenance of artificially created pauperism should be curtailed. This is necessary whether poor law functions are transferred to the county councils or continue to be discharged by parochial boards.

It has always been the opinion of the veteran Sir Edwin Chadwick that the areas of administration should be large. His plan is, that relief should be given within poor law institutions managed according to law by properly qualified officials. The duties of the guardians would then be analogous to the duties of the visiting magistrates in prisons, and the finance and contract business would be done by the councils. It is not of much consequence by whom the law is administered, if only the unjust and mischievous licence which now prevails is abolished.

If there is to be any rearrangement of our poor law system, it is possible we might learn something from Elberfeld in the one particular of nominating properly qualified guardians. If relief were administered 'institutionally' in buildings controlled and managed by the county councils, it might be possible for the council to nominate local visitors for the different unions. Such visitors should be chosen by reason of some fitness for the post. They would have no patronage, and the only inducement to the acceptance of such an office would be some knowledge of the subject and a genuine desire to help the poor. Such a plan has a precedent in the system of local managers in the London Board Schools.

The subject of poor law relief is not a suitable one for the hustings, when the electors are often persons who hope to profit by the distribution of parochial funds. Promises of generous administration constitute the very meanest form of bribery, for the bribe is not even taken from the pocket of the briber, but from the public purse.

CHAPTER XIV

SOME FORMS OF SOCIALISTIC LEGISLATION

WHILE we contend, therefore, that this reform of poor law administration is a matter calling for immediate action, because there is an admirable substitute at hand, it is admitted that the same cannot be said with regard to most of our other socialistic legislation. The reader should observe that the necessity of socialistic legislation has not been denied. A long course of aggressive interference with individual liberty has created a state of things which from time to time could only be rendered supportable by fresh acts of aggression. Lord Shaftesbury and Mr. Forster had perhaps no alternative before them but to substitute for the defective and atrophied sense of parental responsibility the protection to children given by the Factory and Education Acts. What we complain of is that modern politicians show no disposition to watch for and foster a re-quickening of those atrophied instincts of self-protection which have been replaced by the utterly imperfect machinery of regulations and inspectors. It does not appear to occur to them that this is the ultimate goal; and the tendency of the present day is to increase and multiply the duties of the State, and to trust less and less to the individual power of adjustment.

It is our business here to point out some of the imperfections of the State protection of labour. It may not be possible to show exactly how the ineffectual protection now given by the State can be replaced by healthier conditions. It is urged that the opportunity should be sought for, and that, when it arises, it should not be missed.

Before touching on one or two points in which regulative State interference has proved and must always prove to be utterly ineffectual, a word may be said on the interference which is merely prohibitive. In this country a maintenance will always be guaranteed to all by our poor law. We desire to restrict the methods by which this guarantee is carried out, but the guarantee itself must always remain. This fact introduces a new element, and may be held to warrant the State in prohibiting modes of life which fall below a certain standard. The argument is as follows. If left to themselves these lower types of social existence would be decimated by natural forces. The poor law steps in and prevents this. The mere existence of these lower types, as Mr. Booth has remarked, spreads a contagion of difficulty throughout the lower stratum of working-class life. The State will not suffer them to die out. There is therefore some justice in urging that the State should prohibit these dangerous forms of life, and should offer in lieu of them a maintenance from the rates under proper conditions. This extorted admission of the possible necessity of a form of socialism is very characteristic of the difficulty of the situation. The necessity of a poor law is, in practice at all events, axiomatic ; when this is conceded, the prohibitive powers of the State seem to follow. As an individualist one may claim a right to stop here, but there is clearly a temptation to justify also regulative interference with individual liberty, and to run on through the whole gamut of socialistic aggression.

To return, however, to our consideration of some prominent instances of interference by the State which are regulative rather than prohibitive. It is not denied that the Factory Acts (including in this general term all philanthropic legislation in favour of the working classes) have brought about, or at least have been contemporaneous with, a great improvement in the condition of labour. Unless, however, our diagnosis is altogether at fault, the evils which these Acts seek to remove have arisen from former interferences with individual right and liberty. This, however, does not render factory legislation unnecessary. At present statesmanship should chiefly aim at approximating our regulations to that condition of things in which most freedom is given to individual enterprise and liberty, for it is a question whether government by inspectors has not been pushed to its furthest limits.

With regard to the protection given to the young by the Factory Acts proper, and by our compulsory Education Acts, it is probable that these Acts cannot at present be interfered with. If a portion of our population had not been brutalised by long centuries of mischievous socialism, it would undoubtedly be better to leave complete freedom to parents in this as in all other respects. Our State system of education is new and has not yet got much behind the times, but great complaints are already made of the stereotyped uniformity which is required. Improvement only comes by experiment. Yet at present experiment is prohibited, and however great their professional experience and ability may be, teachers are allowed little initiative for the improvement of their own science. Parents are given no choice as to the fitness of the education provided for their children. The claims of mental education have been exaggerated far beyond their merits. Many parents and many schoolmasters are well aware of this, but it is impossible for them to meet and arrange for an experiment of their views till my lords of the Education Office have given their consent.

This event may be postponed till doomsday. So also with regard to the Factory Acts, if intelligent competition were possible, parents who realised their responsibility might meet with employers who were willing to combine technical education and the employment of juvenile labour. Public opinion (a much weaker and less vigilant force than the intelligent competition which a careful father might exercise on behalf of his child) has obliged the manager of a great London theatre to have a school for his pantomime children. Apart from the vexed question whether theatrical life is a good or a bad calling, this resolution of the difficulty points to the direction in which a substitute is to be found for the State control of the lives of the young of our poorer classes. An intelligent father in the artisan rank of life would probably wish his boys to begin technical training before they are free from the present rules of school attendance. Lord Armstrong in some articles in the *Nineteenth Century* Review has exposed with admirable force and unrivalled knowledge of the subject the comparative uselessness of school technical education. It is playing at work. Technical education can be acquired only in the workshop. A widow also requires her elder children to help her earlier than a woman who has a husband to support her. A kind mother, and many widows it is presumed are kind mothers, will give her children technical training while they help her with her work. This training will probably be just as valuable as a knowledge of the names of all the rivers in the kingdom of Spain, without which no poor child can face the Government inspector.

Undoubtedly, however, a repeal of the Factory and Education Acts would throw the young of the labouring class entirely under the control of parents, who have not always a sufficient sense of their responsibility. The proletariate condition into which mischievous legislation of the past has sunk a portion of the working class makes them inappreciative of the value of book education for their children. The State was perhaps bound to provide a system of universal education. We only point out how much more valuable it would have been if the system had grown up naturally and on a self-supporting basis, and also how much more effectually the wants of the working class will be supplied when their own individual liberty, and the enterprise of the teaching profession, can be trusted to play their proper parts.

It may be preferable that all children of the working class should be turned out with their minds contracted to the mould approved by the education code and H.M. inspectors, rather than that they have no education at all. But the system is surely not an ideal one.

These considerations apply with even greater force to the protection afforded to adult labour by the State. Avowedly male adults have never claimed any protection, and if our views are correct it is sincerely to be hoped that the working class leaders will adhere to their policy in this respect. Mines and factories and shipping are, however, under many regulations. Of these no complaint is made, though we may regret that they have been found necessary. The malignant conditions which have rendered inspectors necessary proceed from the same source as the plan now adopted for their cure. Progress, properly understood, should carry us away as well from the socialism which resulted in mediæval injustice as from that which prompts the latest phase of modern philanthropic legislation.

As in the legislation in behalf of the young, the regulations of the inspectors do not go far enough, so here also the protection afforded is not complete; but by occupying so large a portion of ground it has deprived workmen of their power of initiative. Again, there is no guarantee that the regulations are wise and necessary, and the cost of them is undoubtedly prohibitive to a more extended use of the factory system. Whether wise or not, these regulations have tended to drive industry from the factory to the private house, where the evils of what is called sweating most prevail.

This has had two results. *First*, that there has been some curtailment in employment owing to the cost of the system. The costliness of apparatus required by law has increased the tendency towards monopoly, and has thrown the control of business, such as that of shipowning, more and more into the hands of great capitalists. Small people must begin with the inferior class of property, and the system has tended to concentrate rather than distribute property. Shipping regulations are a necessary evil because unpropertied people are not free agents, and but for the State interference the bad owner would be master of the situation.

So also with regard to mines; if men were free agents they might fairly ask to be allowed to sell their skill, courage, and carefulness, for high wages, and to offer to work a dangerous mine. Under the Mines Regulation Act skill and courage, and a reputation for carefulness, are deprived of some of their advantages. The career open to talent has to some extent been closed. The system also raises the cost of many of the domestic necessaries of life, and adds to the burden of taxation and rates.

The *second* result, however, is the most important. The advantages secured by the Factory Acts for the working classes rest too little on their own intelligent competition, and too much on the ubiquitous but not omniscient inspector. Workmen, by the action of the State in their behalf, have been deprived of the opportunity of learning the use of ordinary means to get the more obvious necessities of life, such as healthy houses and a proper sanitation of factories.

As they have not been obliged to learn the first steps so they have difficulty in proceeding further, and are constantly looking to the State to aid them under conditions in which the State is powerless. The working class has gained, no doubt, some of the advantages which the Factory Acts were intended to give, but these Acts have made a break in the continuity of individual effort. They have deprived men of a most invaluable educational process, and this loss perhaps more than balances the gain. Workmen have gained their present position by the short cut of State interference, and they hardly know how to utilise the advantages which they have acquired. The natural course of economic evolution is slower but surer in the end.

For these reasons we are inclined to name the Factory Acts and other similar legislation as one of the causes of the indubitable fact, that although the wages of the working class have increased, and their cost of living decreased by reason of the reduced price of domestic necessaries, yet on the whole their character for thrift and self-reliance, the only effective foundation for continuous progress, has by no means increased in like proportion, if it has not actually in some respects decreased.

Ordinarily, material advantage in this world is gained by thrift and self-reliance. And the gaining of such advantages gives also to their owner a confirmed habit for thrifty and self-reliant conduct.

Thus we return again to the oft-repeated text, that the educational effect of property is of even more importance to mankind than property itself, and that the distribution of property or economical advantages (for it is the same thing) by means of inspectors or committees of management and at other people's expense, by no means gives the same wholesome result as when the acquisition of these has been attained by individual effort.

At the present moment there is some pressure being put on the Government to extend socialistic legislation still further with regard to two subjects, both of them now much before the public. We refer to the so-called sweating system, and to the question of the housing of the working classes in towns.

It has been pointed out with great force that no accurate definition of sweating can be given. Sweating is simply an invidious term applied to conditions of labour which, from one reason or another, seem repellent to the aspirations of civilised life. It is not a matter of sub-contract or an incident in one particular trade such as tailoring, for many sub-contracts, and many tailors and tailoresses are paid on terms of which no complaint is made. It is argued by many persons, and by persons whose opinion is entitled to respect, that a cure for sweating is to be sought in an extension of the system of factory inspectors. It is argued, that if the private houses in which sweating goes on were put under the Factory Acts, the condition of affairs would improve. It is a question, however, whether we have not reached the limit of the inspector system. One reason why the incriminated trades are conducted in private workshops and not in factories is that the inspector system entails a very heavy cost on employers. There is a tendency, therefore, where processes of production are unskilful and therefore unremunerative, for employers of the less competent type to avoid the factory, and to employ the sweater in the hope of making an economy. While the inspector system may perhaps have improved the condition of factory life, it has without doubt extended the field of sub-contract private-house labour, where sweating is most prevalent. It is proposed to go a step further and to prohibit, wherever we can hear of them, insanitary conditions of labour, and to drive the sweating industry away from the sweaters' room into the privacy of the home, where no inspection can successfully follow it. Whether this would be an advantage or not it is difficult to decide. Here is the opinion on the subject of Miss Beatrice Potter, a lady who knows the facts of the case well. In a letter to the *Times*, dated Sept. 22, 1888, she says :—

We must either prohibit home work, or we had better leave the sweating system to develop in its own way. For already the economic conditions of the metropolis severely handicap employers who manufacture on their own premises ; extravagant rent, heavy rates and taxes, high price for coal and gas ; and intensifying all these inequalities, the irregularity of the metropolitan trade, which leaves the responsible employer with serious liabilities during the slack season. If we enforce a higher standard of life in the recognised factory or workshop, if we insist on more space, more sanitation, greater regularity of hours, we shall simply drive the trade into the homes of the people. *The inspection of home industry is impracticable.* The only alternative to a policy of *laisser faire* is to force our workers into the factory system, as we have forced our children into the schools ; *the only radical remedy for sweating is one which will cover the whole area of the disease, which will embrace all labour engaged in manufacture which has escaped regulation.*

The italics are not in the original. There can be no doubt that this exactly states the nature of the problem. The device of appointing additional inspectors, whenever there is a difficulty, is exhausted ; we shall next be asked to prohibit home industry altogether, and this indeed is the alternative which Miss Potter chooses in the next paragraph of her letter. It is impossible to be sanguine about the success of any such experiment. It would be a monstrous thing to prohibit women or men from working for gain in their own homes. The alternative, as correctly stated by Miss Potter, is the *laisser faire* system, a system which is much abused, but which has never had a chance since the beginning of the world.

The objection taken naturally enough to the *laisser faire* system is that it postulates that men are free agents. Under the present conditions of the distribution of property men are not free agents. This may be so, but when we come face to face, as in this matter of sweating, with the ultimate impotence of the State to give to individuals what civilised public opinion wishes them to have, it becomes necessary to have recourse to the despised principle of individual self-assertion and liberty.

We ask no more in this matter than the use of a reasonable opportunism in restoring, or more correctly in giving for the first time, to the individual a chance of adjusting his own affairs. An abolition of out-door relief would remove the rate in aid of wages and bring about a rise in women's wages. Further, it would necessitate the adoption of insurance and thrift as a substitute. This would alter men's habits and character, and would lead them to spend their wages more productively. More clothes and more boots would be worn, and less money consumed at the public-house. The effective demand for common articles of domestic use would be increased. Employment in these industries would be more regular and better paid. Intelligent competition on the part of the workers would be possible, and as it has done in other trades it would in the end raise the status of the now sweated labourer. There is, as far as we can see, no other alternative. If, as Miss Potter suggests, home labour is prohibited, we should have to support almost the entire sweated population by the poor rate, and the vicious circle would be extended.

The evil has been attributed by some to the low price of commodities, and to 'the craze for cheapness.' It need hardly be pointed out that cheapness of commodity is by no means synonymous with a low remuneration of labour. Employers of labour, as well as political economists, are agreed that this is a fallacy. We could give a long list of articles which are now much cheaper than they were formerly, e.g. bread, paper, pins, leather, cloth, oil, sugar, tea, &c. Yet it is clear that the labour employed in preparing these for the market is remunerated at a higher rate than in the old days of high prices. The evils complained of in the sweating system are not caused by the low price of the article sold. The low rate of wages is caused by the redundancy of this particular class of labour, and by the absence of any complete system of trade combination or protection. Even if the retail tailor could sell the finished coat for double its present price, there is nothing in this consideration to oblige him to give more than her present wage to the sweated needlewoman. An employer who hires a labourer to dig a well pays the same rate of wages as a neighbour who hires to dig up a buried treasure. We might with confidence predict that if by means of a trades-union or by more intelligent competition, wages were raised throughout the whole class of slop tailors, the ultimate result would be, not a rise in the price of clothes, but a fall, and for this reason: work which is done by well-paid and intelligent labourers is always in the end the cheapest, especially when these labourers are in charge of elaborate and ingenious machinery. Well paid workmen, working a reasonable number of hours, would enormously increase the efficiency, value, and amount of the work turned out in comparison with the present deplorable system.

Very analogous to the legislation for the protection of labour is the legislation for improving the dwellings of the poor. This last venture in State interference has proved a most gigantic failure. Most of the things which men use in every day life have become in the course of time cheaper, better, and more plentiful. Free trade and competition have given us cheap food, cheap clothes, cheaper locomotion, and all of them of a superior quality to that which our forefathers enjoyed. The working classes have shared in these advantages, but in regard to house accommodation there is no free trade and no competition, and as a consequence constant legislation for the past twenty years has been unable to deal satisfactorily with the condition of the dwellings of the poor. In the country the housing of the labourer entirely depends on the goodwill of the landlord. If he is a benevolent and rich man he builds good cottages, but notoriously he gets nothing like a reasonable return for his money. If the landlord is a poor man, or if he is indifferent to the condition of the labourers on his estate, they have to be content with what they can get. The providing of a cottage at 1*s.* or 1*s.* 6*d.* rent is really a payment in kind of part of the labourer's wages. The system is a relic of feudalism. The landlord, when he lets his land to a farmer is expected to supply labourers *ascripti glebae*, and to pay a part of their wages by giving them house room. The arrangement is open to all the abuses of the truck system. In commercial affairs the standard of currency in this country is gold, yet in the rural districts under the present system the labourer has to accept part of his wages in the shape of house room. The standard of house room may be debased by the inability or niggardliness of the landlord.

In the great towns the building of artisans

dwellings is ceasing to be a commercial undertaking. Our system of land tenure was based on the idea that public policy required permanence of ownership in one family, and our whole political system depended on this.

The State, therefore, has sanctioned and lent its machinery to uphold leasehold contracts extending over generations. When a landlord gives an eighty or ninety years' building lease, he assumes, with the sanction of the State, a power of disposal far greater than that permitted in any other dealings with property. A freeholder's testamentary and settlement powers are limited to the duration of a life or lives in being and twenty-one years, but in a building lease he binds a piece of land to a definite use for ninety years. He exacts very onerous covenants from his tenant for the purpose of keeping the property in good repair. But public opinion, rightly or wrongly, has made it very difficult for a landlord to enforce these covenants, especially during the latter part of a lease, when it is most necessary, and in cases where a low class of house property is concerned. As a matter of fact, tenants have not generally been obliged to observe their covenants to the ground landlord in this respect. Towards the end of a building lease it is not the tenant's interest to repair, and public opinion not unnaturally will not allow a landlord to force his tenant to spend money on improvements which will not be exhausted during the term of the lease. Property held on this system of dual ownership is doomed to deterioration.

But it would be an exaggeration to say that all insanitary habitations are due to the leasehold system. Our English system of land tenure is rotten to the core. In the debate on May 1, 1889, on the Leasehold Enfranchisement Bill, it was shown that many working class dwellings built on freehold land were, if anything, worse than those which had been erected on building leaseholds. There is an entire absence of competition in the business of supplying artisans' dwellings, and we question very much if our reformers are on the right track in their search for a remedy. The restriction of a leasehold system and the general immobility of all tenure in land has, without doubt, been one cause of the present congestion, but the long dissociation of our proletariate from property, more especially from property in land, has accentuated and rendered permanent the evil. The law has so long deprived them of any chance of getting land and house room on the same terms as they get their bread and their clothes, that they imagine the thing to be impossible.

An unnecessary confusion is introduced into the discussion by talk of the 'natural monopoly of land.' By this it is meant that there is only a limited supply of land. This, however, is equally true of bread and cheese, and every other commodity under the sun. Mankind, when taking its own domestication in hand, has to recognise the natural limitation of supply. The limitation is very elastic in its nature, and varies as the sources of supply become developed and accessible to human use, and nothing is more elastic than the ability of land to carry a population. The natural monopoly of land, or, to speak more correctly, the variable state of a country's development, should have proved a natural regulator of the growth of the population; and if the principle of private property had been allowed to have full play, the progress of population would have been controlled proportionately to the development of land and the other economic resources of the country. Unfortunately, tribal and then feudal socialism thought that land could be put to a better purpose, just as to-day Mr. George and his followers think that land is best employed in paying all the taxes rendered necessary by the cost of government. Our contention, on the contrary, goes to show that the adjustment of population to wealth can only be successfully and equitably accomplished when the tenure of property, especially of such an important item as land, is made accessible and mobile, and when individuals are allowed to protect themselves by it, and to guide their conduct and the increase of their species by reference to it.

Mr. George's proposal for the endowment of paternal government by confiscating all property in land will not find much favour with those who estimate at its proper value the benefit of paternal government. The gratuitous supply of locomotion at the charge of an endowed government is a favourite item in Mr. George's proposals, and has a specious air about it. It would be worth considering, if we knew that progress was at an end and that human ingenuity was played out. For if Government had been enabled to supply gratuitous travelling in stage coaches at the charge of the land revenue of the country, there can be little doubt that we should still be travelling in stage coaches, and that the railway would never have been invented, or, if invented, would never have been adopted in the teeth of the vested interests protected by the State.

The control of the wealth of the world should belong to the living, and not to the dead or to the unborn. Wealth distributed by means of private property is used for the benefit of the living, who best know the uses to which it should be put.

The dedication of property to public purposes by means of endowment, is not a device productive of much benefit to mankind. It is difficult to get an impartial judgment on the policy of the endowment of middle and upper class education, for most of us have been brought up within its influence.

We fear that in the main it has been inimical to progress. Antiquated theories of education, which some might call obscurantism, have sat very heavily on our public school system. The general result is not such as to make us wish to endow Government, and to entrust other and important interests to its care.

In every alteration of law a controversy arises as to the equity to be meted out with regard to existing contracts. If we pass by this familiar difficulty as incidental to all reform, we are impelled to follow our argument to its logical conclusion, and to look for a remedy in the entire withdrawal of Government interference with regard to contracts about land. Herein lies a drastic, but perhaps the only effective, reform of our system of land tenure. Government should simply refuse to enforce any contract whatsoever with regard to land. A landlord would have to receive payment in advance, or else trust entirely to the good faith of his tenant. Under these conditions the ownership of land would very quickly follow its use. The user and the owner would be the same person. By such a bold return to first principles the whole system of burdening land to carry out the wishes of former owners would be swept away. No former owner, whether dead or alive, could then by mortgage or settlement restrict the free flow of property in land. If a landlord required money he would have to sell his land; he should no longer have the power to deprive the community of the value of a mobile piece of wealth by entangling the title in a mortgage or settlement.

The enfranchisement of leaseholds, the prohibition of settlements, the powers given to life tenants to acquire the fee simple of their holdings are very cumbrous methods for repairing the errors of the past. Government, going, as we now argue, far beyond its province, guarantees to owners of land the enforcement of all sorts of inconvenient and impolitic contracts. The simple and direct remedy is to abolish this guarantee.

Free trade in town building land is at present, from one cause or another, absolutely impossible. The system has established a most effective monopoly. In olden days artisan dwellings were built in the central parts of London; these have got out of repair, yet the leasehold system was prohibitive of rebuilding. If there had been freedom of trade they would have been rebuilt one by one. Good landlords would have got good tenants at a remunerative rent, and areas might have remained working-class quarters. Under the present system, after a time the condition of the houses became intolerable, clearances had to be effected by the Metropolitan Board of Works. The owners rather welcomed this intervention. Extravagant compensation was paid. It followed that while it does not pay a man to sell bad boots, it yet pays a landlord to have his houses condemned by the public authorities.

When a large clearance was made, naturally the area became available for manufacturing purposes or for a superior class of dwellings, thus the value of the site was enhanced. The Board, however, was obliged to forego any profit from their operations as the area had to be devoted to artisan dwellings. The ground was then sold far below cost price, as a rule to some semi-philanthropic body like the Peabody trustees.

The Peabody trustees, being under no obligation to make a commercial profit, provide accommodation and let at a rent which defies competition from the commercial builder who has to make a living out of his trade, and any spark of enterprise which may survive among the landlords of the neighbourhood is effectually extinguished.

The contribution from the rates in reduction of the rent of artisans' dwellings built under these circumstances is manifestly a rate in aid of wages, and a portion of the rate is of course collected from the persons who have still to linger on in unimproved quarters. The benefit obtained in this way is entirely illusory. The cleared areas are not readily covered again with improved dwellings, the delay is very great, for the conditions do not invite commercial enterprise to rush in. There is one

East end area at least which cannot be covered with dwellings on any terms, and which has been declined as an open space by the parish vestry. Increased overcrowding is the result. The system, as Mr. Spencer says, has produced 'first bad houses, and then a deficiency of better ones.' The burden of the rates incident to this system, and amounting in London to nearly one-third of the rental, is a further impediment to the provision of good houses at a rent suitable to working-class incomes.

Impotence has fallen on the whole system, and the cry is now raised that Government should build upon as well as clear the areas.

We are approaching fast to the condition of Cholesbury in Buckinghamshire, where in the old days of the poor law the rates failed to meet the charges imposed on them, and where every one except the parson and the farmers was a pauper, with wages paid out of the rate-fund, which at length went bankrupt. We cannot refrain from quoting the summary of the position given by Mr. H. Spencer :—

The policy initiated by the Industrial Dwellings Acts admits of development, and will develop. Where municipal bodies turn house-builders, they inevitably lower the values of houses otherwise built, and check the supply of more. Every dictation respecting modes of building, and conveniences to be provided, diminishes the builder's profit, and prompts him to use his capital where the profit is not thus diminished. So, too, the owner, already finding that small houses entail much labour and many losses, already subject to troubles of inspection and interference, and to consequent costs, and having his property daily rendered a more undesirable investment, is prompted to sell, and as buyers are for like reasons deterred, he has to sell at a loss. And now these still multiplying regulations ending, it may be, as Lord Grey proposes, in one requiring the owner to maintain the salubrity of his houses by evicting dirty tenants, and thus adding to his other responsibilities that of inspector of nuisances, must further prompt sales, and further deter purchasers; so necessitating greater depreciation. What must happen? The multiplication of houses, and especially small houses, being increasingly checked, there must come an increasing demand upon the local authority to make up the deficient supply. More and more the municipal or kindred body will have to build houses or to purchase houses rendered unsaleable to private persons in the way shown, houses which, greatly lowered in value as they must become, it will in many cases pay to buy, rather than to build new ones. Nay, this process must work in a double way; since entailed increase of local taxation still further depreciates property. And then, when in towns this process has gone so far as to make the local authority the chief owner of houses, there will be a good precedent for publicly providing houses for the rural population as proposed in the Radical Programme,[1] and as urged by the Democratic Federation; which insists on 'the compulsory construction of healthy artisans' and agricultural labourers' dwellings in proportion to the population.' Manifestly the tendency of that which has been done,

[1] *Fortnightly Review*, 619, 620, Nov. 1883.

is being done, and is presently to be done, is to approach the socialistic ideal in which the community is sole householder.[1]

In a note Mr. Spencer adds:—

If anyone thinks that such fears are groundless, let him contemplate the fact that from 1867–8 to 1880–1, our annual local expenditure for the United Kingdom has increased from 36,132,834*l.* to 63,276,283*l.*, and that during the same thirteen years the municipal expenditure in England and Wales alone has grown from 13,000,000*l.* to 30,000,000*l.* a year.

He quotes Mr. Rathbone's authority, *Nineteenth Century*, Feb. 1883, for the statement that local taxation in New York has risen within his, Mr. Rathbone's, experience, 'from 12*s.* 6*d.* to 2*l.* 12*s.* 6*d.* per cent. on the capital of the citizens, a charge which would more than absorb the whole income of an average English landlord.'

A considerable number of artisans are finding their way into the suburbs, where the conditions of the trade do not entirely prevent the builder seeking customers by providing a good article at a moderate cost. To prevent this solution of the matter, Parliament for many years has imposed a passenger duty tax, and artificially raised the cost of locomotion. It next obliges the railway companies to run a few workmen's trains at an unremunerative price, and remits the tax on this portion

[1] *Man versus the State*, 36.

of the traffic. Government first makes locomotion dear, then, finding that the working class suffers from this, it taxes the rest of the community in order to give workmen a very insufficient supply of an article which they would have got in the ordinary course of business if Government had only refrained from meddling. In this way the natural adjustment of a free population in dwellings such as they can afford, is let and hindered, and day by day the rates and the cost of all this incompetent management drives further and further away the chance of poor men getting what they want through the ordinary channels of trade.

One sees on a small scale the result of establishing a Government monopoly in land in the recent disclosures of the Metropolitan Board of Works. The board failed to remove the evils complained of, and by a natural principle of deterioration common to all associated gatherings of men, it developed in the exercise of its function of landlord into an institution worked by wire-pullers in the interest of an inner circle of corrupt members and extortionate, peculating officials.

The feudal system had its patriotic and chivalrous instincts; relatively to the time these instincts corresponded to the philanthropic impulses of the modern agitator. The principle of deterioration has many phases, but it is a question if the tyranny and brutality of feudalism would not be preferable to the universal landlordism of a bureaucracy like the late Metropolitan Board of Works.

In fairness to the arguments of the *laisser faire* school, it should be observed that the principle has never had a chance. The principle of individual adjustment to environment is the principle of progress, and the history of mankind is the disentanglement of the individual from slavery, custom, superstition, and the aggression of socialism. There is no golden age in the past. There has been action and reaction, and in the main the balance of gain rests with the individual. The Community extinguishes the Individual. The Community hardens into the Manor. The Imperial Government, on the plea of giving protection to the individual, absorbs and destroys the jurisdiction of the manor. Again, in our day Parliament avows its incompetence for universal management, and preaches the doctrine of devolution. Grand Committees, County Councils, Home Rule are the fashion of the day. The great fetich is overworked, it therefore turns out upon us a lot of minor fetiches, and the vulgar turn to them reverently as panaceas for all our disorders. In a generation we shall find out the incompetency of our new tormentors. In the meantime we can only pray that their powers of mischief will be stayed.

CHAPTER XV

THE ETHICAL ASPECT OF THE QUESTION

In the foregoing chapters, we have endeavoured to follow the subject in the dry light of facts. Reference to ethical and religious considerations has, as far as possible, been avoided, for the introduction of terms of moral praise or blame tends only to obscure the question. Men are very much what their circumstances make them, and their conduct is entirely relative to the environment to which their character has become fitted.

In insisting on the importance of this aspect of the question, we are not blind to the great value of the principle of altruism. This title is given to the force which we now seek to describe, because it enables us to include under it the opinions of two different, and to some extent opposing, schools of thought. First, there is the view of the ordinary church-going public. They rely for any possible regeneration of society mainly on the altruism which arises in response to the call of religious duty. Second, there is the altruism hoped for by the pure socialist, which is totally different. It has nothing of asceticism in it. It arises from no effort of self-sacrifice. Individual life is entirely merged in the idea of society. Social instincts have become dominant. Individual organisms have coalesced to form the organism of society. Action is no longer self-regarding but society-regarding, for self has no meaning for man except as forming a portion of the society in which he moves.[1]

These two schools attribute a far greater *material* power to unselfishness, to what the socialists call social ethic, than is its due. Altruism is not a lever by which, in the present state of human character, a great revolution can be worked. Let us consider first what we have rather loosely called the ordinary churchgoers' view of the question.

The old-fashioned theory was that the poor must be with us always. The well-to-do should labour to alleviate the suffering of the poor. The poor should be patient. Under the teleological theory of religion, an appeal is made to the argument from design. These inequalities of wealth were created for the purpose of giving rise to the virtues of compassion and patience. This was the utmost reformation possible. To-day the public has got much more in earnest about the matter, and aims at a larger amelioration of the condition of the poor. The majority of unthinking people, however, in renouncing the old limited

[1] See Belfort Bax, *Ethics of Socialism*.

view of the possibility of reform, have not renounced the old methods of alleviation, or to speak more correctly, they over-estimate the force of the old method. Compassionate action, or altruism, was an adequate weapon in the old ideal of alleviation, but it is quite inadequate to the root-and-branch reformation which is the ideal of the present generation. We have already dwelt on the aggravation of the difficulty, introduced by the action of the promiscuous benevolent. Many persons, however, who see the folly of indiscriminate almsgiving, are yet very loth to part with the old faith in the efficacy of altruism. The view which they hold is less logical than that of the pure socialists, but it certainly has a more practical air. Self-renunciation and altruistic benevolence have been experimentally proved possible. No one can dispute for a moment the vast amount of good and heroic work which benevolence has done; no one can wish to see its action fettered or narrowed. It is difficult, however, to see how men can persuade themselves that altruism is a lever of such universal application that society can be reformed by it. It is true that the professors of this creed do not often explicitly declare that the disorders of the world can be cured by those who, having prospered in the battle of life, can afford to exercise benevolence; but they are so enthusiastic over their panaceas, and so often intolerant of those who urge them to a closer study of social and economical facts, that their practice in effect makes them liable to the charge. It is of course the business of clergy and teachers of morality to urge men to be just and generous in their buying and selling, in their paying and taking of wages, but stubborn economic facts will not yield to this treatment. A good employer may feel very keenly for the toilsome ill-rewarded lives of his operatives, but if he wishes to avoid bankruptcy, he cannot pay the wages which he would like to see his workpeople earning. He can treat his people courteously and considerately, and he can minister to their comfort and amusement in many ways. But as to the scale of wages he is practically powerless. A farmer in the olden days employed his labourers at the current rate of seven shillings or eight shillings a week. If he was a good sort of man he was kind to them and did what he could for them. A modern farmer may be a coarse and ill-tempered master, but he has to pay twelve shillings or fifteen shillings a week for his labour. The unselfishness of the two men has nothing to do with the status of their labourers.

A favourite proposal of this school is that the public should give their custom to employers who obtain in some way a certificate for benevolence, and that illiberal employers of labour should be boycotted. The practical difficulty about this is that it is impossible to trace the history of manufactured goods before they come to the retail shop. Nor is it very easy to see how a tribunal for the issue of such certificates could be elected. Philanthropists are not remarkable for their knowledge of business. The system would give rise to much agitation and levy of black mail. It would lead the enterprising tradesman to issue odious advertisements of his own benevolence; and generally the proposal is not one about which it is possible to be enthusiastic.

There is, however, another ground for deprecating the view which looks to altruism as the principal lever for raising the status of the poor. It assumes a permanence of the present situation, and attaches far too little importance to the dignity and independence of human life. We have said that ethic is relative to material conditions. The poor have been excluded from the enjoyment of certain material advantages, and from the ethical character which these advantages render possible. It may be that the office of securing independence is only a natural instinct, and should not be dignified with the title of virtue. It is, however, obvious that, until a certain measure of independence is secured, there is no room for the practice of some of the higher virtues of civilised life. Consider, for example, how many virtues depend upon the possession of a home. Decency, cleanliness, the love of wife and children, hospitality, and the proper use of leisure, are all qualities which have their origin in the home. Even the fine arts owe their existence to the desire of men to beautify the furniture and decoration of their homes. We might even go further, and say that until a man has secured competence for himself and his dependents the whole field of altruistic virtue is forbidden to him. A poor man, who is generous and unselfish outside his own family, incurs not unreasonably some suspicion of recklessness.

The inoculation of the masses with the instincts of property might on this reasoning be held to be, not perhaps a necessary, but at all events an auxiliary condition to the development of the higher forms of ethical character.

We shall see the force of this argument more clearly when we consider the ethic which is said to be the basis of socialism; to that side of the question we now turn.

It was not till after the early chapters of this book had been written and completed, that a volume of essays by Mr. E. Belfort Bax, entitled 'The Ethics of Socialism,' came into the author's hands. It was surprising to find that he makes essentially the same analysis of the early forms of society as that made in the opening chapters of this book.[1] He draws, it need hardly be said, con-

[1] *Ethics of Socialism*, 9.

clusions exactly the opposite of those contained in the present text. He finds that primitive society, and therefore ethic, rested on kinship. 'The society, by the very fact of its own development, merged into the state.' Property, however, was a disintegrating influence, for 'no sooner had personal property become definitely the basis of social order than the naïve ethical sentiment of early society was at an end, and an individualistic ethic had taken its place' (p. 10). 'The old feeling of duty of the *ought* still survived, but without its old object and without its old basis' (p. 11). The new ethic of socialism is a regeneration of this primitive feeling. Its object is now not the kindred, but society at large. He illustrates the operation of the new religion by the story of a Parisian national guard, who fights and dies *pour la solidarité humaine.*

The disintegration of the communistic tenure of property, and of the naïve ethical sentiment which it produced, is thus a phenomenon of which it is possible to take different views. The theory of Mr. Bax, a representative socialist, is quoted, as it enables the issues to be presented to the reader more clearly. Mr. Bax is undoubtedly right in seeing in this crisis a conflict of the principles of individualism and socialism. We naturally prefer our own interpretation, namely, that in the feudal system the dead hand of an abortive form of socialism seized on the property of the country and tried to make mankind conform to its ideal; and that, from this and other similar manifestations of the same principle, a vast legacy of disaster has been entailed on human kind.

The socialist view, as expressed by Mr. Bax, is that the 'naïve ethic' and the communistic tenure were of the true type, and that disorder has come because of the invasion of the principle of private property and individualism. It does not seem to deny that history is a chronicle of the advance of this invasion, or, as we have called it, of the gradual and painful disentanglement of the individual from the trammels of communism. Private property and individualism have, however, in his view produced such evil results, that the time has come for the re-introduction of the archaic principle of communism. The communism of the village community and of the primitive family is the only historical sanction for this view. So slight a precedent can afford no historical basis for socialism; nor does Mr. Bax, except by way of illustration, appear to claim this for it. Socialism, if anything, is the preaching of a new Evangel, an inspired invitation to society to make a leap in the dark.

For as we understand it, Mr. Bax is prepared to launch the social revolution under the guidance of the new ethic. The point is worth dwelling on. In their analysis of the existing framework of society the socialists are naturally very successful in tearing a passion to tatters. Every one admits that the time is out of joint and the socialist is more vehement in his denunciation than any one else, but when it comes to be a question of declaring a constructive policy, plain men find it very difficult to discover what it is they propose and on what principle they rely. Mr. Bax's book, the most intelligible work on socialism which we have come across, argues that we ought to make society rely on the new religion, the new ethic of socialism. It is absolutely necessary for socialists to put forward some such principle, for with human nature as it is at present it would be manifestly absurd, a proposition too ridiculous for discussion, to say that Government can organise all industry, give work to everyone, and yet not become bankrupt. The Post Office may be a very admirably managed institution, but obviously it only gives employment to the number of hands required to carry out its work. There probably are a great many people anxious to become postmen and letter-sorters and who cannot get engaged by the Postmaster-General. The same state of things would occur under the socialist régime in all the other trades managed by Government, unless human nature is going to be altered. They believe, as we do, in the theory of evolution, and they profess to see in socialism some power of altering human nature to its environment, such as we believe exists only in the principle of individualism. This power of adjustment will arise, they hold, from the universal adoption by mankind of the ethic of socialism.

What then, we are eager to know, is this new ethic? It consists in the realisation of the idea that ociety is not merely an aggregate of individuals. 'As soon as society exists at all,' says Mr. Bax, 'ethical sentiment must also exist explicitly or implicitly.' A social environment gives rise to the social ethic or character in the individual, or, to quote Mr. Bax, 'the ethical sentiment is the correlate in the ideal sphere of the fact *of social existence itself in the material sphere.*' We are not concerned to dispute Mr. Bax's theory of the metaphysic of ethics. Much of it appears to be very ingenious, but it is difficult to see its relevancy to the matter under discussion. Ethical sentiment is a fact which we all admit. It forms a part of a Christian as well as a socialist theory of society, but though it arises out of the mere 'fact of social existence in the material sphere,' it has no absolute control over the laws which regulate evolution in that material sphere. Mr. Bax's contention that ethic is correlative to material conditions, and that 'The ethic bears the impress of the particular society whose ethic it is' (p. 4), is precisely the view which we have been at pains to express throughout this volume. There is an ethic arising out of the material conditions of poverty. Reform must operate on both relative and correlative. It may be that socialist and individualist have the same ideal before them; the question is, what are the means of attaining to it? Our argument has been that the goal can only be reached by gradual individualistic development. The socialist appears to think that by an effort of altruistic ethic the material conditions of society can be reformed. This we believe to be a delusion.

The socialist ethic can make an enthusiast willing to die *pour la solidarité humaine*, but it cannot alter the fact that two and two make four, or that human life has a tendency to come into existence, without much regard to the maintenance provided for it. The individualist is not indifferent to the value of the socialistic ethic; on the contrary, he regards it as one of the most wonderful adjustments that arise out of man's correlation to society. When man's intercourse with his fellow men is conducted without friction, a certain mental pleasure is begotten in him. The desire of attaining this frame of mind becomes very strong. At times this desire is called our social conscience, or, in socialistic language, the enthusiasm of the new ethic, but it must not be confounded with the material conditions which render it possible, if they do not actually give rise to it. Under the present condition of inequality, the new socialistic ethic does not exist. Even the national guard who dies *pour la solidarité humaine*, had a short way of dealing with the bourgeois and capitalist class, and in his chapter on men *versus* classes, Mr. Bax admits this. 'Meanwhile we who live to-day, who are the offspring of a class society, and who breathe the atmosphere of a class society, bear ineradically the mark of the class demon upon us' (p. 105). Mr. Bax's own book is full of complaints of the stupidity of mankind and the wickedness of the bourgeois. This is precisely our point; if all men were good and wise, and would adopt Mr. Bax's ethic without more ado all would be well, but we know perfectly well that they will not. We know that the primitive apotheosis of a class ideal of society bound men down to centuries of serfdom. If we did not know on the clearest evidence what was the condition of mankind under the feudal system, it might without doubt be made to appear a socialistic utopia. There was no private property in land; each class in due subordination had its place and duty assigned to it. Everything existed *pour la solidarité nationale. La solidarité humaine* has a finer sound, but one sees no reason to believe that a working class bureaucracy would escape from the deterioration which converted the village community into the feudal manor.

In this world of reality we require some more common-place, more homespun principle on which to trust for the proper management of the world's affairs. The enthusiasm *pour la solidarité humaine* may be a bright flash of prophetic insight; it cannot be an ethic such as Mr. Bax describes till, as we contend, individualism has brought about an harmonious adjustment of individual claims. The correlative to this material condition of society may be the ethic of which socialists dream. At present no such ethic exists, for there is no state of society out of which it can arise. Mr. Bax appears to confuse the cause with the effect, the flower with the root.

The socialistic ethic can only arise when individualism has so adjusted character to environment that the main objects of socialism have been achieved. A socialisation of property, as proposed by Mr. Bax, would only lead to a new dominion of class. The equality and happiness which he and all of us desire can only be founded on a more complete individualisation of property. This process, as we have seen, creates the instincts correlative and necessary to itself, and leading to a harmonious adjustment of the whole framework of society, makes the social ethic a possibility and not a prophetic vision.

Mr. Bax insists very strongly on the fact that the conduct resulting from the socialistic ethic is automatic and not ascetic, and arises naturally out of man's existence in society. He is fond of disparaging the ascetic ideal of life, the ascetic poison as he terms it (p. 20). He 'grudges the amount of energy required to be expended by the individual in his effort to acquire self-discipline.' This is a logical conclusion from the confusion of cause and effect which seems to vitiate the whole theory set out for us by Mr. Bax.

Self-sacrifice, altruism that is not automatic, is a fact, the possibility of which is proved beyond a doubt. Mr. Bax disparages it, and compares it disadvantageously with some ideal of his own.

The more ordinary orthodox view, on the other hand, exaggerates its importance, and imagines it to be an archimedean lever by which the world can be moved. It may be difficult to make a correct analysis of the fact that men do take philanthropic interest in the affairs of fellow men whom they have never seen. The feeling is so ancient, so universal, that it may be the development of some instinct bequeathed to man by some prehistoric ancestor. It may have grown correlatively out of the fact that man has necessarily been a gregarious animal.

In any case it is an influence which is used with very great effect in human affairs, but it is not an unerring guide. As reasonable beings we require to study the conditions under which associated life can be made most supportable. It is then our business to try to attain these conditions, and to make our altruism as well as our selfishness both contribute to this result. Unfortunately, we shall find that altruism can act only within certain limits; it cannot, either by inspiring the State or by acting in committees and societies, do much to improve the condition of the poor. By such conduct it runs the very great risk of increasing the degradation into which the poor have fallen.

It is the business of the reformer to make the advantages of civilised life available for the poor. Property is the main condition of civilised survival. The destruction of the poor is their poverty, their want of property. It is the business of altruism, therefore, to help the poor to acquire property by all lawful means, and thus to inoculate themselves with the instincts of property. We have endeavoured to show that on moral as well as material grounds this is the line of social reform to which all effort should be directed.

Sympathetic and friendly endeavour should be made to direct the attention of the poor to the real nature of the problem. The English poor have a passionate love of independence. A great deal might be done by men of leisure and education, who are not working men, if they would assist their poorer neighbours in perfecting their system of saving and insurance; in this latter field there is an immense amount to be done. As yet the poor have received little or no assistance from the benevolent in this respect. On the contrary, they have been lured away from independence by the well-meant but degrading administration of out-door poor law relief. The rich, too, can help the poor in their endeavour to compete intelligently with the economic difficulties by which they are beset. The term intelligent competition covers a great deal. It means a due development of the trade-union proper, of the natural trade-union of the family; it means a careful husbandry and a wise expenditure of wages.

This policy of helping the poor to help themselves makes much larger demand on the time and labour of the rich than the simpler process of doling out relief to the helpless and hopeless. The most important service which men of business and means could render to the working class, would be to place on a sound commercial basis the question of insurance. If commercial enterprise could raise the burial club into the life insurance society, one of the most difficult problems of working class life would be solved.

These views are not new, but unfortunately they have not been much followed. Philanthropists are not often good men of business, and also they have been too much occupied by the engrossing business of the relief of distress. It is, of course, very desirable that distress should be relieved by careful and considerate almoners, but these more important, and, we venture to think, more useful fields of activity should not be ignored.

There is much useful work being done by devoted men and women, but their work would not suffer if social questions were more intelligently considered. There is without doubt need of more enlightened views of the causes and remedies of pauperism.

It is a melancholy reflection that, as a rule, each generation, each tyro in the administration of poor law and charitable relief, insists on disregarding the warnings of his predecessors, and on gaining his own experience, too often at the expense of the independence of the poor. Human error travels in a circle. Modern philanthropy in its hot fits not unfrequently shows a disposition to carry us back to the degradation of the old poor law.

Public opinion is now engulphed in a wave of humanitarian sentiment. It is difficult for a writer to get a hearing if he is not able to propose half a dozen infallible panaceas. We have here no panacea to offer, but have only to urge the unpalatable advice, that the student of social phenomena should avail himself of the dry light of historical and economical research.

For EU product safety concerns, contact us at Calle de José Abascal, 56–1°, 28003 Madrid, Spain or eugpsr@cambridge.org.

www.ingramcontent.com/pod-product-compliance
Ingram Content Group UK Ltd.
Pitfield, Milton Keynes, MK11 3LW, UK
UKHW040226290926
15471UKWH00001B/21
* 9 7 8 1 1 0 8 0 0 3 7 0 4 *